A Christian Teenager's GUIDE to surviving high school

by Ashley Conner

with commentary by her little brother, Zachary

Market Square BOOKS

A Christian Teenager's Guide
to Surviving High School

©2017 Market Square Publishing Company, LLC.
books@marketsquarebooks.com
P.O. Box 23664 Knoxville, Tennessee 37933

ISBN: 978-0-9987546-5-9

Library of Congress: 2017958677

Printed and Bound in the United States of America

Cover Illustration & Book Design ©2017 Market Square Publishing, LLC
by Kevin Slimp

Editors: Lucy Akard Seay and Kevin Slimp

THE HOLY BIBLE, NEW INTERNATIONAL VERSION®, NIV®
Copyright © 1973, 1978, 1984, 2011 by Biblica, Inc.® Used by permission.
All rights reserved worldwide.

Table of Contents

Introduction

I never expected to become a published author. What started out as a private blog for my little brother, Zachary, became the basis for this book after a publisher discovered our blog.

The idea for the blog came to me when Zachary was about to begin 9th grade. I remembered how stressful it could be to navigate the sometimes-rough waters of those four years of high school.

My brother and I have always been close, and I simply hoped my advice could make his high school career a little less stressful and a little more rewarding.

This book is limited to nine chapters, so not everything from the blog is here. But you'll get all my best advice and the highlights of my suggestions about almost every area of high school you can think of.

In the past four years, I've enjoyed watching my brother grow from an awkward 9th grader into a mature, confident high school senior. On top of his growth in confidence, he has also grown in stature, shooting up a full 12 inches in the last year!

Although high school can be scary, it doesn't have to be. As I said, Zachary seems to be turning out well! I'm not sure if my blog had anything to do with that or not, but I think it really did make his entrance into high school a bit easier.

Now, please allow me to welcome you to this public version of my blog! Whether you are a rising 9th grader or already a graduating senior, I truly believe you'll find this book helpful and encouraging.

Thanks for reading!

Ashley Conner

Chapter 1

The School Year Begins

Primer

Since you're reading this book, chances are you either received it as a gift, you're part of a group studying the topic of high school survival, or you picked it up because you saw the title and thought you could use a little help navigating the years known as "High School." Whether you're a freshman feeling nervous about the first day of school or a senior embarking on the final year of pre-adulthood, high school can intimidate even the most confident teenager.

What do you think is the most intimidating part of starting a new year of school?

What is one thing you can do to prepare for your new school year?

FRESHMAN

My Freshman Year: The first days

I remember the first day of high school like it was yesterday. It was nearly impossible to fall asleep the night before. I had spent hours picking out the perfect outfit for my first day. I woke up early to make sure I had plenty of time to shower and do my hair and makeup. I desperately wanted to fit in with the hundreds of new faces I would encounter as I walked into my high school for the first time.

A few hours later, I found myself staring down the sidewalk toward the school doors. Confident senior girls strolled into the building. They seemed so much older than I was. They hugged each other and smiled as if they hadn't seen each other in years. As I saw the way they dressed and related to each other, I was overwhelmed with the reminder that I was an awkward kid transferring from a tiny middle school to a huge high school. In my blue t-shirt and jeans, I began to feel like I was dressed for a Blue Man Group audition instead of Day One of high school. At first, I wanted to run back to my mom's car and rush home for a change of clothes, but the line of cars at the drop-off wouldn't have allowed me to make it back in time, even if I had seriously considered such a mad dash. My only options seemed to be:

a. Hang my head and sneak into the school unnoticed

b. Do my best to look like I fit in

I flipped a coin in my brain, pulled my shoulders back, and pretended to be confident as I walked through the front doors.

At first glance, high school was even wilder than I had expected. The lobby was filled with students, hundreds of them, bumping shoulders as they hustled to pick up their schedules and find their classes.

I knew only two people at my new high school. One had transferred from my middle school, and the other I knew from my church youth group. I breathed a huge sigh of relief when I saw Bridget, my youth group friend, standing against the back wall. She was probably just as relieved as I was.

We grabbed our schedules and wandered off to find our classes. Having a terrible sense of direction, I wound up in the wrong classroom more than once. Teachers looked at me with pity as they pointed me in the right direction. Things didn't get much better over the next few days.

I continued to get lost as I looked for my classes. I prayed I would figure everything out eventually. I had been part of a very small class at a very small middle school, and our teachers hadn't adequately prepared us for the shock awaiting us in high school. Once, after noticing I was lost, an older student walked with me to my classroom, saying," Don't worry. It all seems new right now, but you'll have it down in about two

3

weeks." I didn't believe her at first, but after two or three weeks, I actually was able to find my classes all by myself. I could check that off the list.

At the end of the first month, I noticed my confidence growing. I had made a few friends and had learned enough to navigate the hallways without too much trouble. Even so, my freshman year came with its own share of challenges. Sometimes, it was lonely. After the first few weeks of school, I had made at least one friend in each of my classes. When one of them was absent, though, I was back to being the kid nobody knew.

My friends from middle school probably wouldn't have recognized me. I'd gone from outgoing, energetic, and well-known to lost and often alone. I didn't have close friends to share girl-talk with at sleepovers or to walk with me around the track during P.E. There were days throughout my freshman year when I felt isolated, when I couldn't understand my classmates' inside jokes, and when I felt totally out of place as the new kid. I knew, however, that I could eventually figure this out.

One thing I loved was the idea that during my freshman year I could totally re-create who I was. Without close friends in any of my classes, every minute was a chance to remake myself into who I wanted to be. I've since come to realize that it's possible to re-create yourself at any time, not just when entering a new school. It's something I wish I had learned earlier, but thankfully, I was able to embrace the idea as I entered this new adventure called high school.

When I began middle school, I was known as a quiet, smart kid who kept her head down and was often the teacher's pet. I took time for me to find my place and gain confidence. It was like starting over in high school, and I knew it was again time for a change. I began to interact more in class and to make friends with students I never would have hung out with in middle school. I joined Key Club, started working at a local gift shop, and even auditioned for the school's musical theatre program. I continued to be involved in my youth group at church. It was one of the few places where my group of friends remained relatively constant. In addition, the adult leaders were people I had grown to know and trust throughout my middle school years.

Freshman year was difficult because it was the first time I ever had to let go of old friends, but it was also a time when I realized I could still be friends with classmates from my middle school even if they had moved on to other high schools.

It was a year of feeling like an outsider. It was also a year of making new friends. Most importantly, freshman year was the time when I learned I could accomplish whatever I set out to do, even if it scared or intimidated me at first. It was the year that broke the ice and helped me realize my adventure was just beginning. When you think about it, the opportunity to remake yourself from scratch is incredible.

I learned that hesitation wasn't for me. If I felt like joining a football game, I did it (even though I was a terrible athlete). If I felt like bringing pizza rolls to lunch every day, I decided I would bring pizza rolls to lunch every day. There was no limit to who I could be or what I could do. I was learning to take advantage of this gift.

Life Hack:

What I learned as I began my freshman year

Your first year of high school is a time to be fearless. There's no need to worry about what other people might think. It's the perfect time to blaze your own trail. Don't be afraid to make new friends.

Be courageous, especially if there's something new you want to try. Say yes to opportunities. Ask for what you want and practice being a leader instead of a follower. Freshman year builds the foundation for the rest of your high school experience, so make it great from the beginning.

At the same time, hold on to people and activities from your past. Stay grounded. So many students seem to drop out of youth group as they enter freshman year. High school is a busier time than middle school, and it's easy to let things like church and youth group go by the wayside. I'm really glad I didn't.

My best advice is to stay involved. You'll be thankful in the future. As you navigate the sometimes-stormy waters of high school, you'll be more secure if you hold on to a solid foundation.

Reflection _____ questions for freshmen

What are/were your top two fears about becoming a freshman in high school?

1.

2.

SOPHOMORE

My Sophomore Year: One of the best so far

My sophomore year of high school was one of my favorites. The newness of freshman year had worn off, creating room to relax and have fun. I had made several friends and finally understood the layout of this huge building. There had been a giant learning curve, but by my second year of high school, it wasn't nearly so scary.

I had come from a middle school class of only 18 students to a high school with a student body of more than 2,000. As a sophomore, I was still too afraid to eat the cafeteria food (you'll have to trust me on that), but at least by then I could walk into the lunchroom without feeling intimidated.

Most sophomores reading this book probably go to a smaller school than I did. With more than 2,000 students in the school, naturally the cafeteria was a big place. Finding a table with friends was a skill I eventually perfected during my freshman year.

My second year of high school was a comfortable middle ground. As a sophomore, I enjoyed the feeling of not being the "new kid" anymore, without the pressure of college being right around the corner. It was also a great chance to make friends with younger students, because now I understood what it was like to be in their shoes.

During the first few days of your sophomore year, you'll have the opportunity to befriend younger students who are facing fears similar to those you experienced when you were beginning high school. You'll probably run into younger friends from your church or youth group who will see you as a "grown-up" who can help them navigate their first days as freshmen. Make the most of this opportunity.

Like much of high school, sophomore year comes with challenges of its own. New friendships emerge, some old friendships go by the wayside, and dating becomes more commonplace, providing opportunity for even more drama.

I'll write more about dating later. For now, let me offer one quick word of advice: Don't let dating become too high a priority.

Sophomore year can be so much fun. Don't add drama where it's not necessary. As you get older and start to meet people with whom you just seem to "click" with, it's normal to lose touch with your old middle school friends. During our freshman year, my middle school friends and I banded together to survive the newness of high school. In our sophomore year, however, after realizing we had actually made it through a year of high school, some of us branched out to try new things and make new friends. In time, it was natural that a number of early friendships were set aside to make room for new ones based on more current interests and high school activities.

It may feel like you're doing something wrong when you start to lose touch with old friends, but the reality is that life changes, and that's okay. Sophomore year is a great time to make new friends who might be around for years to come.

It's also a time to become even closer to longtime-friends who share your interests. Once you've decided whom to hold onto and whom to let go, your remaining friendships will become even more meaningful.

Life Hack:

Your Sophomore Year: First step to college

One thing I wish someone had told me earlier in high school is that sophomore year is the time to begin looking at scholarship opportunities for college. Junior year is all about applying to colleges and getting accepted, taking the ACT, and upping your GPA as much as possible in the span of 12 months. It's a lot to take in, and it's easy to forget about scholarships in the jumble of so many activities and responsibilities.

Even if you don't start applying for scholarships as a sophomore, find out what's available and decide which scholarships might be worth your time. Local scholarships are fantastic opportunities because you'll always have a better chance of being selected from a smaller applicant pool. If there's a major scholarship you want to shoot for, sophomore year is a great time to work on it.

This early in the game, you've got adequate time to prepare a killer application, giving yourself the best chance of being successful. Most importantly, never sell yourself short with the "it's too early" excuse. Free money is free money, no matter how early it arrives.

Once your junior year rolls around, you'll be glad you took an early look at scholarship options. You'll be able to relax on the sidelines while your friends are caught up in the stress of college planning.

9

Reflection

Have you lost any friends from your time in middle school? How do you feel about that?

What do you feel is the biggest difference between freshman and sophomore year of high school?

What did you learn during your freshman year that can make your sophomore year even better?

JUNIOR

My Junior Year: Moving closer to adulthood

Speaking of college planning, welcome to your junior year of high school. This is the year you'll answer three important questions. Trust me – you'll hear these a lot:

How did you do on the ACT/SAT?

Where are you going to college?

What do you want to major in?

First Things First: Standardized Exams

By your junior year, you'll have received countless emails and pamphlets for ACT or SAT study courses, and you'll begin to notice test prep books while walking around bookstores. After a while, it starts to feel like your entire future is wrapped up in test scores. You'll begin to wonder why adults act like this one exam determines the course of your whole life.

The answer, you will be relieved to hear, is that it doesn't. How you score on the SAT or ACT does not define who you are or predict how your life will unfold. That was not a typo. Your entire future does not hang on the score you earn on college entrance exams.

What do these tests really mean? Universities use standardized test scores to evaluate high school students for admission. In reality, though, your hobbies, extracurricular activities, and overall grades matter just as much, if not more, than your standardized test scores.

Earning an average or below-average score on your first

11

SAT or ACT doesn't mean you are an average or below-average person. It just means you haven't yet found the study method that works best for you. Don't get me wrong. Now that I'm in college, I realize more and more how important it was to do my best in my high school classes. Unfortunately, however, I might have worried a little too much about my grades and test scores. We'll discuss this in more detail in a later chapter.

If you have the option, it's good to take standardized exams more than once. I took the ACT three times, for example, and my score increased by seven points from the first to the third test. If you're like most students, your score will improve each time you take one of these exams, so plan to take them several times. If you've done your best, but exam performance just isn't your forte, then simply emphasize your stronger qualities when completing college applications. Scoring lower than you expected on a standardized test is not the end of the world—not even close.

Instead of emphasizing your SAT score, for example, write about your experience as treasurer of student government. If you have a part-time job in high school, be sure colleges know about that, too. Keep in mind, college recruiters are people, just like you, and they undoubtedly remember what it was like to juggle school, a job, and other responsibilities.

If you are working to assist your family financially or to help pay your own way through college, find ways to highlight that, too, as you complete applications. Filling out forms gets old quickly, but don't let that keep you from doing your best to represent who you are and what you've accomplished in high school. When describing your participation in various clubs and activities, let college recruiters know how serious you were about helping these organizations thrive. Hone in on your soccer skills, perhaps, and focus on the leadership abilities that come with being a student athlete.

While it is extremely important to do your best on the SAT or ACT, your personal admissions applications are a golden opportunity to let colleges know what really sets you apart. Your value as a person is not based on your standardized testing skills. Yes, the exams are important. Yes, you should study. No, you shouldn't stay up every night worrying about what will happen if you don't score in the top one percent.

The College Question: Juniors hear it a lot

The next question you'll be confronted with is: "Where are you going to college?" For some people, there's an easy answer. For example, I grew up 30 minutes down the road from the largest state school in Tennessee, so for me, it was a no-brainer. For others, it's a little trickier.

My best friend goes to college in Kentucky, because that was the only place where she could study equine business. She is passionate about horses, and pursuing a career in equine business meant moving to Louisville, Kentucky. I know what you're thinking. If she's serious about horses, she must be rich. No – far from it. She arranged trade-offs with a local stable during high school, which allowed her to learn a trade while getting the riding experience she desperately desired.

At the end of the summer after our high school graduation, she packed her suitcase and said goodbye to her family, friends, and dogs. Then she took off on the adventure of her lifetime, thanks to several well-deserved, hard-earned scholarships. In the beginning, she was lonely and afraid. Living on your own for the first time can be exciting—and scary.

As a high school junior, looking ahead to this not-too-distant reality can be intimidating. Don't worry. Just like I experienced in my freshman year of high school, within a few months, my best friend hit her stride. Now, three years later, she has a beautiful apartment, fantastic roommates, and a circle of great friends. She relates well with her professors and is heavily involved in campus activities. Because she was willing to take a risk and go for the school she really wanted to attend, life is going pretty well for her.

Choices! Choices! Choices!

When you're selecting a school, there are a few major factors that come into play:

How far are you willing to go?

How much can you afford?

What do you want to study?

First, decide how far you're willing to go. Whether you prefer 100 miles or 1,000 miles away, grab a map and draw a circle around all the territory within a certain distance from your home. Look closely within that circle. What are your options? Take note of all the colleges and universities that fall within that circle.

Then, it's time for the question many high school juniors don't think about: How many of those schools can you and your family afford? In high school, teachers and guidance counselors sometimes tell you that you can find a way to afford any school through scholarships and loans. It's true; financial help is out there. But you need to understand that this help is limited.

Your education is incredibly valuable, but it will be much less valuable if you find yourself in debt for the next 20 years. If your parents or someone else will be helping with your college expenses, talk with them about what is reasonable.

Try not to feel like you're entitled to go to school in Europe simply because your best friend is going to Oxford.

Finally, what do you want to study? If you don't know yet, that's perfectly okay. You'll have plenty of time to decide later. On the other hand, if you already know beyond a shadow of a doubt that you want to spend your career as a marine biologist in Alaska, then you should plan to head north. Consider all the colleges and universities that offer the degree you'd like to pursue. In the end, if they're more than you can afford or further away than you'd like to go, then you'll need to reevaluate what you plan to major in. Eventually, you'll narrow down your choices to a few schools.

Junior year is all about exploring your options, dreaming big, and then deciding what your future will hold for the next four years. No matter how overwhelmed you might feel, take a deep breath and relax. As important as this decision seems right now, try to remember that nothing is permanent.

It's really okay if you don't know yet exactly what you want to study in college or do after college. You'll figure it out eventually, even if you experience a few changes along the way.

But it seems like everyone else knows what they want to do

Since middle school, my best friend knew she wanted to be an equine business major, studying at the University of Louisville. Her life seemed to be right on track. I had no idea what I wanted to do as an adult, and that was totally intimidating for a long time. In the end, though, we both wound up in college majors we love.

15

She took the path of following her passion. I took the path of randomly picking a route and finding my passion along the way. It worked out perfectly for both of us.

Is there someone at home, church, or school whom you feel comfortable asking for advice as you begin looking toward your post-high-school years?

Life Hack:

Your Junior Year: Big decisions

In the end, junior year is about deciding what's right for you in the present. Your college major will probably change— and probably more than once. It's okay if you don't pick the perfect major or the perfect school the first time around.

No matter what you decide right now, your life is not set in stone. It is an adventure waiting to happen. Kick back, take a deep breath, and enjoy the ride. Junior year is also about being brave. Much like when you entered your freshman year, it's about having the courage to look intimidation in the face.

The source of intimidation may have changed from navigating high school to preparing for college, but the challenge is much the same. I handled it, and so can you. Bring it on.

Reflection

Name someone at home, church, or school whom you feel comfortable asking for advice as you begin looking toward your post-high-school years.

If you could ask this person one question about life after high school, what would it be?

How is your faith developing as you near your last year of high school? Are you letting church activities slip to make time for other activities?

SENIOR

Senior Year: King (or Queen) of the Hill

Hello, senior year! This is what you've been waiting for. You made it through the dreaded freshman year. You enjoyed the relative calm of your sophomore year. Junior year was a blur of college preparations and standardized testing, and you survived. You're finished. No need to read any further.

Just kidding!

Don't forget—you still have one more year of high school to complete. Senior year may be the most exciting year of all. If you haven't already, you'll soon be applying to one or more colleges. Or maybe you're planning to enter the military or move straight into a career. Whatever your situation, you've got one foot out the door even now.

What comes next?

My senior year of high school was simultaneously one of the easiest and hardest years of my life. On one hand, I was working four nights a week, often getting home around midnight and crashing until it was time to rush back to class the next morning.

On the bright side, however, class was a cinch, I had friends all over the school, and there was almost always a movie night or party going on at someone's house on weekends. Things were going pretty well. Yes, I was burning the candle at both ends. But, after all, it was senior year, and time was precious.

There are things to do; there's fun to be had; and there are worlds to conquer. During your senior year, adults will probably be regularly telling you it's the best time of your life. If I could go back and give myself one piece of advice, it would be to relax more and work less.

Don't get me wrong—work is a good thing. But don't work so hard that you constantly feel stressed about your schedule. Take time off occasionally and find ways to prioritize your friends and family along with your job. Senior year is one of the last years of your life when you can really let go and enjoy the financial freedom of living at home, along with the convenience of having all your friends in one place.

Right now, that may not seem like a big deal. But trust me—a few years down the road, you'll wish you'd spent more "quality time" with your loved ones.

I had a bad habit of working too hard and stressing too much. I probably got involved in too many activities and spent just a little too much time with friends as well. After all, it was my senior year.

I remember my dad telling me not to worry so much about grades and work. Now I realize there was a lot of truth and wisdom in what he was telling me. If you have siblings, senior year is a great opportunity to spend time with them before heading off to your new life after high school. My younger brother is a senior in high school now (how did that happen?), and even though he's running around with his friends much of the time, the days he's at home are some of my favorites. Part of what makes them so special is knowing that he'll be heading out on his own new adventure in just a few short months.

Celebrate your senior year. Live each day to the fullest. Find joy in your classes. There's a good chance you'll actually miss some of those teachers later on. Laugh often. Take a road trip. Hug your mom. This is the year you've worked for, and this is your chance to go out with a bang.

What about church?

As a high school senior, it's easy to get so involved with friends, school events, and work that other priorities such as spending time with your family and staying plugged in at church can easily take a backseat.

It's not unusual for parents to allow a little more freedom as their seniors prepare for life after high school. It's likely they've realized you're going to be in college or in the work-force within a few months, so they might be letting you spread your wings a little. Let me offer a bit of advice: As busy as you are, don't pull away from church during your senior year.

It's easy to let this happen; but once you start to pull away, it's a hard habit to break. Realize that you have a certain responsibility to remain active in your church and youth group. When seniors pull away, juniors often follow suit.

Your senior year is the perfect time to step up and be a leader among your group at church. Your continued involve-ment could pay long-lasting dividends for both you and other youth who follow behind you.

Life Hack:

Senior Year: No regrets

After you've moved on to college or the workforce, you will often look back on the accomplishments of your senior year. Don't look back in regret.

Complete your classwork. Stay close with your family. Don't pull back from church activities. Remember, there is life after high school. These things will pay dividends as you move further into adulthood.

Make your senior year as special as it can be.

Reflection _____ questions for seniors

What scares you most about life after high school?

Have you become less active in church and family activities as you're nearing the end of high school?

21

If you had your entire senior year to do over again, what would you do differently?

What advice would you give to incoming freshmen and sophomores about their remaining years in high school?

What could you do right now to make the most of the time you have left in high school?

Reflection _____ questions for everyone

Hebrews 12:1-2a (NIV)

[1]Therefore, since we are surrounded by such a great cloud of witnesses, let us throw off everything that hinders and the sin that so easily entangles. And let us run with perseverance the race marked out for us, [2]fixing our eyes on Jesus, the pioneer and perfecter of faith.

The author of Hebrews compares life to a race. In many ways, school is also like a race. We learn to pace ourselves in the early years to prepare for the steep hills ahead in middle school. By high school, much of the race is behind us. Still, it's importance to keep our focus as we run toward the goal of graduation.

As you endure the final phase of your school career, what can you do to keep your eyes on the goal of graduation?

What can you do that would help you fix your eyes on Jesus during the busyness and confusion that comes with high school?

A Word From
Zach

I don't always agree with my sister, but she was right about the start of high school. Like her, I have felt the stress that comes along with new classes, teachers, and friends.

I'm already learning that the high school years go by fast. Be sure to enjoy the time while you can.

Oh, and don't forget your pencil on the first day of class. That's a lesson I seem to learn every year.

Chapter 2

So there's this teacher
who doesn't like me

What teacher has had the most positive influence on you up to this point?

Have you had any teachers who you felt didn't like you (for whatever reason)?

If you did, how did you handle the situation?

All Grades

Not everyone is going to like you

During my sophomore year, one of my teachers didn't like me, and it rocked my world. I tried to be pleasant in her class, I always turned my homework in on time, and I didn't act out (too much) during her lectures. No matter how hard I tried, though, this woman wasn't having any of it. She often called me out in class without reason and made me the butt of jokes that weren't really meant to be funny.

Having been a teacher's pet for most of my first ten years

of school, not being well-liked was a new one for me. I wish I could tell you the story had a fairytale ending, in which an eventual heart-to-heart conversation made everything better. In reality, however, we just survived an awkward semester of being in class together, and that was that. No fuzzy goodbyes at the end of the year or "I'll miss having you in my class" conversations. We had a distant relationship, and when I graduated, I forgot all about her. (Well, not totally, since I'm telling you about her now.)

My dad is a conference speaker. Once, I heard him tell about the best and worst teachers he had in school when he was growing up. His worst was an English teacher he had during his junior year of high school.

For this story to make sense, there are some things you need to know about my dad. He grew up in a poor family, and he started working when he was twelve years old, delivering newspapers. By high school, he was working in a grocery store. Most days, after school, he would rush off to work. Even in high school, he was working around 30 hours each week.

As my dad tells the story, this particular teacher apparently didn't like him because he didn't put enough effort into his homework and papers. She had no idea my dad was doing the best he could with the little bit of time he had.

In the middle of his junior year, Dad's entire class was required to take an IQ test. Toward the end of the school year, everyone's IQ test score was posted on the wall outside the school office. (I'm sure no school would get away with that today.)

Dad told me he remembers taking that IQ test because he finished so quickly. The person in charge of the test thought he had just answered randomly so he could finish the test and leave. You can imagine his English teacher's surprise when the results came back and Dad's IQ was the highest in the class. She was furious.

In front of his entire class, she told him, "I always thought you were stupid. Now I realize you were just lazy!" She went on to tell him he would never pass college English. He laughs when he tells the story now, because she was right. His college entrance scores were so high that he received two years of college English credit without having to take the classes.

When Dad shares this story with groups, he always tells them about his favorite teacher, too. Mr. Rogers was his English teacher the following year. One day, Mr. Rogers asked Dad to stay after class to visit for a minute.

He told Dad that he should be a writer. My dad thought he was joking, but Mr. Rogers insisted he wasn't. Dad says that's why he's a writer today, and now people all over the world read his work.

Although it wasn't easy to understand at the time, I learned a very important life lesson from my difficult teacher: Not everyone is going to like you, and that's okay. This is true not only of teachers, but also of friends, workmates, and others with whom you'll come in contact. At the end of the day, the important thing isn't whether or not you can convince them to like you; it's whether or not you can let it go and move on.

As a people pleaser, I continue to struggle with this reality. Generally, if I think someone doesn't like me, my natural reaction is to go out of my way to convince that person that I'm nice or to bend over backward trying to be a friend.

Despite my good intentions and best-laid plans, this method rarely seems to work for me. It generally just wears me down and leaves me feeling even less likable than before.

Also, I'm learning that sometimes when I think someone doesn't like me, I'm actually misinterpreting things. In the case of my teacher, I later learned she had become completely burned out with teaching. She retired the next year.

In many instances, you are not the problem. You just get caught in the line of fire. It's helpful just to accept that not every relationship will be full of warm fuzzies.

There are times, however, when someone truly may not like you as a person, even when there's no good reason. That's just reality. In those situations, I've learned that sometimes the best response is simply to move on.

Reflection _____ questions for everyone

What do you think? How might you deal with a teacher who seems to dislike you for no reason?

With my classmates, I could expend all kinds of energy trying to get even with someone for not liking me, or I could try to change this person's mind. I learned it's usually best to let bygones be bygones, then move on to more important things.

During my senior year, there was one girl I just seemed to rub the wrong way, no matter what I did. I tried to befriend her, but she simply didn't like me. Thankfully, we only had one class together, so it was easy enough to avoid her, but her low opinion of me was obvious.

My initial reaction was to try to change her mind. I was overly kind, going out of my way to do nice things for her and stressing out when she didn't return the favor. After nearly a year of trying and failing, however, I finally accepted the fact that she didn't care for me and probably never would.

Life Hack:

You can survive having someone dislike you. It's not fun, but it's part of life.

Life happens. I'm not the first author to write those words, and I won't be the last. Our goal should be just to roll with the punches of life as well as we can.

In the back of my head, I keep remembering one of my mom's best pieces of advice: "Never burn a bridge if you can help it."

Even if you're never going to be friends with someone, there's no reason to be mean. Do your best to be civil when you have to interact, and if necessary, avoid the person as much as possible. However, you never know when you might run into him or her in the future, so it almost always pays to be nice.

If you have a teacher who doesn't like you, hang in there. You'll have another teacher soon enough, and that next one will probably like you just fine.

Reflection _____ questions for everyone

Matthew 5:43-45 (NIV)

[43] "You have heard that it was said, 'Love your neighbor and hate your enemy.' [44] But I tell you, love your enemies and pray for those who persecute you, [45] that you may be children of your Father in heaven."

How can you apply this Bible passage to your relationship with a teacher who seems to dislike you?

What does it say about you if you only express kindness to teachers and schoolmates who already like you?

Romans 12:18 (NIV)

[18] If it is possible, as far as it depends on you, live at peace with everyone.

A Word From
Zach

It's difficult to imagine, but as likable as I am, there actually have been students at my high school who didn't like me. I've lucked out, though, because the older I've gotten, the more my peers have seemed to like me after all. Also, now that I'm in my senior year, I find that I don't worry so much anymore about who does or doesn't like me.

Sometimes I have to admit that my sister is right. Just as Ashley has already written, I've found that kindness is infectious, and I've learned that over time those people who disliked you the most seem to become your friends in the end.

There's yet another bright side. High school doesn't last forever. Soon enough, I can put anyone who doesn't like me in the rearview mirror... and so can you.

Chapter 3

Actually, nobody likes me...

So you've had the teacher who didn't like you (and you survived), but what happens when it seems like nobody likes you?

The reason for this feeling can change a lot from year to year, but loneliness is universal. We all feel it sometimes, and it's never fun.

Have you ever felt like no one at school likes you?

Has making friends become easier or harder over the years?

How do you feel about the upcoming school year? Excited? Anxious? Scared to death?

FRESHMAN

Newness can be lonely

My freshman year of high school was incredibly lonely at first. Making friends isn't always easy, and it's normal to feel intimidated by the process. It requires determination to find people who really click with your personality.

At the beginning of my freshman year, it felt like everyone else in the school had already made friends or had a giant friend circle around them. In class, sometimes it was hard to find a partner for a project or someone just to talk to, because so many of the other students already knew one another.

Newness can be lonely, but it's also an opportunity. As a freshman in high school, there were two things that helped me find the courage to make it through the year:

First of all, remember the story of Daniel from the Bible? King Darius throws him into a den of hungry lions because Daniel won't stop worshiping God. An angel rescues Daniel by protecting him from the lions throughout the night. When the king comes back in the morning, he's shocked to find Daniel still alive, and he celebrates the work God did in the lions' den.

So how is this story relevant to your life as a freshman in high school? Well, let me share with you one of my favorite Bible verses, which happens to be found in this story. After Daniel has been rescued from the lions' den, the king asks him what happened.

Darius has had trouble sleeping because he couldn't stop thinking about Daniel overnight. Finally, at first light, he rushes to Daniel and basically asks, "How is your God keeping you alive?"

Daniel's response stuck with me throughout my freshman year, as well as through other tough spots in my life since then.

> "My God sent his angel, and he shut the mouths of the lions. They have not hurt me, because I was found innocent in his sight. Nor have I ever done any wrong before you, Your Majesty."
>
> **Daniel 6:22 (NIV)**

35

This verse resonated with me when I was a freshman because I felt exactly like Daniel as I walked into high school for the first time, alone. Though my situation was perhaps not quite as deadly, I still felt as if I were heading straight into a lion's den. The building was full of new people, unfamiliar places, and a lot of uncertainty.

I repeated this verse in my head as a mantra through the first couple weeks of my freshman year. If God could shut the lions' mouths and protect Daniel, then how much more could He help me survive the newness of high school? He'll help you, too. No matter how big or scary the situation may feel in the moment, you will find a way to handle it. Hang in there. I'm living proof that it can be done, and I think you'll find that facing high school gets easier over time.

The other thing that helped me so much in making it through those first few weeks was reminding myself that I'd already accomplished harder things.

In your life, too, you've already succeeded in many challenges. High school is just one more thing to figure out. At this point, you've already made it through elementary and middle school, worked on plenty of papers and projects, done odd jobs, and made many new friends. This is just one more challenge, and you can handle it.

And, if you keep trying your best and nothing is working, sometimes your doctor or a professional counselor is a good resource. It's important to remember you are not alone. There are people who care.

Life Hack:

You can do this!

The beginning of high school may not be easy, and it may be lonely, but you've overcome greater obstacles. You've made it this far, so why stop now? Once you're familiar with the building and some of the people in your classes, everything will fall into place.

Remind yourself that no matter how tough it may seem at first, everything will be easier in a couple of weeks. Just keep rolling with the punches, and before you know it, you'll have this thing figured out!

Reflection _____ questions for freshmen

What has been your greatest obstacle since you began school as a young child?

What obstacle might you face during your freshman year of high school? How can you plan now to overcome it?

SOPHOMORE

Losing touch with old friends

By the time you're a sophomore, high school isn't nearly as intimidating as it was just a year ago. You've survived your freshman year, and you aren't a brand new student anymore. Another plus is that it's too soon to start stressing about college. Life is pretty good.

A challenge of sophomore year, though, is that your friends from middle school may start losing touch. You'll probably hang on to a few of your closest friends, but it's normal to lose contact with those who move on to different schools or even those at your school who become involved in classes and activities that are different from the ones you have chosen.

Sophomore year is the first time I began hearing phrases like "true friends" and "friends of convenience." Friends of convenience are people whom you might be very close to for a short time, but after a while, you begin to realize you don't have as much in common as you thought.

Not all of your close middle school friends will remain close, now that you're more acquainted with high school and don't need each other as a safety net any longer. Even if your friend group feels a little off-kilter, don't worry. Soon things will fall into place.

On the other hand, sophomore year is a great time to start meeting new people. You'll be more familiar with your classes at this point, and you'll have a better idea of what you're looking for in new friends.

For me, sophomore year was a time to dive into activities

I really enjoyed and to make friends with others who shared similar interests.

Some things I tried were a perfect fit, and some weren't. (It's official: I will never be a professional athlete.) In elementary school, just being in the same grade pretty much filled the requirement list for a friend. In middle school, the list of requirements grew, but friends who liked the same movies or had the same hobbies as I did fit the bill. My list of friend requirements suddenly took a turn, however, during my sophomore year.

As a sophomore, I joined my school's musical theatre program and fell in love with performing. I made new friends who loved to read, laugh, have thought-provoking coversations, and play Disney trivia board games. The year went from being one of the loneliest, at first, to being one of my favorite years of high school.

Sophomore year was also the year when dating became a little more prevalent, as other high school friends began to drive and spread their wings a little.

Life Hack:

It's okay if things feel a bit strange.

Whether you're in the dating scene as a sophomore or still on the sidelines, it's good to remember that high school relationships are usually short-term, so it's important to keep up with your group of friends.

At some point in your sophomore, junior, or senior year, it's possible you will begin to date. When that happens, make sure you're still saving plenty of time for friends and family. At the end of the day, breakups are no fun, but they're much less lonely if you've maintained a few close friendships.

In a nutshell, sophomore year is a great time to figure out who you really want to be in high school and to cultivate close friendships. It's fun to discover new hobbies and talents and to build on relationships you started during your freshman year.

Reflection _____ questions for sophomores

Now that your freshman year of high school is behind you, what is the biggest change you expect to experience during your sophomore year?

What can you do to maintain close relationships with your family and friends during your sophomore year?

JUNIOR

About life after high school

Junior year should just be called "College Applications 101," because that's basically what I remember most about my junior year. It is the year of deciding what you want to study in college, where you want to go, and whether you want to stay close to home or go it alone in a far-off place.

If you feel overwhelmed or lonely in this planning process, you're not unique. You are surrounded by a class full of intimidated and nervous future collegians, so don't think you're in this by yourself.

Taking college visits and thinking about what lies ahead can sometimes make your junior year feel like your freshman year all over again. As you consider what you'll be doing after high school, this may be the first time you're faced with a decision that nobody else can make for you.

Instead of college, you may be thinking of entering the workforce or the military after high school, but that probably doesn't make planning for the future any easier. Many of your friends will be taking off for higher education, internships, or jobs, and now it's up to you to figure out your own plan. Things sure seemed so much easier in middle school, didn't they?

But here's your chance to remember what we've been practicing since freshman year. Take a deep breath. Relax, and remind yourself that you can figure this out.

One of my most vivid memories from my junior year is when I began my first real job. I'd worked easy, five-hours-per-week jobs since my freshman year, but my junior year was the first time I started working significant hours. That was a big change.

It takes a little while to adjust to junior year, because it's the first time you and many of your friends may have a lot going on outside of school. Your best friends won't always be free to hang out on weekends, and you'll sometimes have to prioritize work or homework over social activities.

It's important to recognize that even though junior year can be incredibly busy, your friends will still be your friends, and your family will still be your family. Even if you miss out on things now and then, your close friends and family will still be around.

On the flip side, junior year doesn't have to be all work and no play. In spite of college applications, jobs, homework, and extracurricular activities, make sure to prioritize yourself sometimes. That can be hard to remember in the midst of band practices, ROTC, club meetings, sports, and everything else you'll have going on. Promise yourself you will find time to answer "yes" to invitations to hang out with friends and family now and then.

During my junior year, I began to notice my relationship with my family evolving. My parents were used to having me available 24/7. All of a sudden, they had to consider my schedule when making family plans. Looking back, I realize I wasn't the only person in my family who had to make serious adjustments as my high school career drew closer to an end.

As your schedule fills up and your life gets busier, make it a priority to be considerate of your family and friends. They still need you. You might not have as much time as you once did, but you are just as important to them as you ever were.

Life Hack:

You are growing up.

No matter how tight your friend group is, things will change as everyone develops new priorities. It may feel like a juggling act sometimes, but junior year is a year of figuring things out, and it's great practice for growing up.

This is a year of planning for what comes ahead, but don't worry too much. You've still got a life in high school, you've still got friends and family, and you still have one year to go. Make the most of it!

Reflection _____ questions for juniors

How do you feel about your junior year of high school? Are you more excited about the possibilities or nervous about the responsibilities?

What can you do to ensure you maintain close relationships with your family and friends during your junior year?

SENIOR

Don't miss the best parts

Welcome to the pinnacle of your high school experience. You've worked long and hard for this, and now you're finally here. Yay!

Senior year is the best. At least, that's how I felt. You've got the high school thing down, and you know exactly what you're doing. Enjoy it as much as possible, and be sure to take time to appreciate having all your friends and family in one place this year.

You've probably been thinking about life after high school already, but this is the year you will seriously focus on high school graduation. No matter how many times you tell your friends and family you're "so sick of high school" and "can't wait to get to college," the end of high school is coming, and there will be a lot you will miss.

Don't waste time on college tunnel vision, the way some of your classmates might. Senior year is amazing; take advantage of it while it lasts.

When I was in high school, my mom loved being involved in as many of my clubs and activities as possible. During my senior year, I began to realize that she was going to miss her time as the parent of a high school senior. Dad wasn't always excited about driving me to soccer practice or dance class when I was in elementary school, but during my senior year, he seemed to miss those times. I began to realize that senior year was a time of change for my parents, just like it was for me.

Most of the year, though, I found myself battling serious

"senioritis." I was so ready to be done with high school and move on to the next thing. I had been there, done that, and was ready to take on the world. Throughout my senior year, I completely took for granted all the fun afternoons when my friends came over to eat popcorn and watch movies or to lie on a blanket in the backyard and talk about the mysteries of the universe. (Just kidding! We mostly talked about chocolate ice cream and boys.)

When the end of high school rolled around, I stopped dead in my tracks. People were packing bags and saying goodbye. It happened much too quickly. All of a sudden, I realized I wasn't ready for high school to be over.

Whether you're running for the door with your bags packed or having a hard time saying goodbye, make sure to enjoy every moment of this year. It's exciting to be moving toward the amazing adventures ahead, but don't forget about the fun taking place in your life right now!

Life Hack:

Make the most of this special time in your life.

The end of your senior year of high school requires accepting newness all over again, the way you once did as a freshman. Thankfully, though, I've got some good news.

Remember how you had no idea what to do on your first day of high school, but you figured it out? You know how that seems like only yesterday, and now you're here at the end of your senior year? See, you've done it once, and you can do it again.

Make fun memories, meet lots of friends, and don't be afraid to have lots of exciting adventures. You're going to have the best time, so stop worrying so much about what's ahead. Don't sweat the small stuff. This is the time of your life. Get going!

Reflection questions for seniors

What can you do to make sure you don't get too over-whelmed during your senior year?

What can you do to avoid catching "a major case of senioritis"?

How can you keep your faith and church activities as priorities when life starts to become really busy?

All Grades

Reflection

Read Daniel 6:16-23.

In the Freshman section of this chapter, I mentioned that Daniel 6:22 is one of my favorite Bible verses. In the story, an angel rescues Daniel by protecting him from the lions throughout the night. When the king returns in the morning, he's shocked that Daniel is still alive.

For me, beginning high school was a lot like being thrown into the lions' den. It difinitely got easier over time, but took a lot of work and prayer to overcome the challenges.

Has there been a time in your life when you felt like you were being thrown into the lions' den?

How did you handle that experience?

Daniel approached his situation in such a way that King Darius noticed Daniel's faith and was so inspired that he commanded his entire nation to revere the God of Daniel. How can you handle the obstacles you face this year in such a way that others are inspired by your faith?

A Word From Zach

In elementary school, I ended up by myself a lot, even though I didn't want to be. Most days, I would sit under a picnic table on the playground during recess, digging a hole in the dirt.

In middle school, I continued to hang out alone much of the time because I didn't know how to make friends.

Once I entered high school, though, I learned the simple truth: Finding new friends gets easier as our confidence grows. I gradually learned how to introduce myself to others, and things seemed to work out from there.

When it comes to making new friends in high school, joining clubs and taking electives are good ways to find people with common interests. Joining the band during my freshman year was one of the hardest decisions of my high school career. I heard discouraging comments, like "it takes all your time" and "you have to stay after school every day." But I loved band, and I learned that sharing experiences, whether social or school-related, is a great way to make friends.

I went back to my elementary school a couple of years ago. You guessed it — the hole is still there.

Chapter 4
Parents: the Good, the Bad, and the Ugly

Primer

One of the most embarrassing moments of my high school career happened the first time I was invited to hang out at my friend Taylor's house.

Let me set the scene, so you'll get the full picture: After graduating from a tiny private middle school and moving on to a giant high school, I struggled to find my way as a small fish in a big pond. Most of the other kids came from feeder schools and had known each other for at least a couple of years.

Taylor was the very first friend to invite me over to her house, and I was thrilled to have someone to hang out with outside of school.

I knew I had one shot to make a good impression. If she liked me, maybe I could work my way into her group of friends. This day had to be perfect.

When I arrived, her dad wasn't home, but her mom lived just down the road, so we walked back and forth between the two houses, picking out different board games.

We finally settled at her dad's house for a while, playing with the dogs and battling it out in *Disney Scene It*. Then my mom called.

"Are you at your friend's house?"

"Yes, Mom. We're playing board games."

"Okay. Is her dad home?"

"No, but her mom is. She lives down the road. Is that okay?"

"I guess...."

We talked for a couple more minutes, and then I hung up,

forgetting all about the conversation.

An hour later, however, there was a knock at the door. My friend and I looked at each other nervously. Nobody was supposed to be here…. Was it a burglar? A kidnapper?

All of a sudden, I heard my mom's voice, calling for me from the front porch.

"Are you there, girls?"

A few years later, I realized my mom really did have my best interests at heart; she was trying to keep me safe. In that moment at Taylor's house, though, I would've traded Mom for a burglar in a heartbeat.

After an awkward introduction between my concerned mom and confused friend, we walked down the street and introduced our parents, confirming that there truly was an adult at home nearby. I laughed it off in front of my friend, but when I got home, I was seething. How could my mom embarrass me like that in front of my first high school friend?

Thankfully, the story had a happy ending. Taylor breezed through the awkward moment, which we quickly put behind us, lost in an afternoon of pizza rolls and games. We stayed close throughout high school, and she actually ended up as my first college roommate.

My relationship with my parents had some pretty severe ups and downs during my high school years, which I now realize is a common phenomenon for many teenagers. Your relationship with your parents will go through various stages as you grow up and prepare to head out into the real world.

The key is to be prepared for what's ahead and hold on tightly. Otherwise, you're in for a pretty bumpy ride.

What are some "growing pains" you've experienced with a parent, another family member, or friends?

What have you done to work through some of these growing pains in a healthy way?

FRESHMAN

You're not in charge yet

As a freshman in high school, you'll probably rely pretty heavily on your parents. That is totally normal and to be expected. They probably still pay for the majority of your food, clothing, and other expenses, since you don't have a driver's license yet.

There's a good chance their schedules revolve around you, for the most part, making sure you arrive on time for school and extracurricular activities, then picking you up at the end of the day.

When you're a freshman, your parents are key players in keeping you happy, healthy, and safe. Your level of responsibility is fairly minimal at this point, and that's okay. Family obligations tend to increase as you grow into adult life.

There are a few important things to remember about your parents at the beginning of high school.

1. Your parents are still in charge.

As a 21-year-old, I wouldn't expect my mom to show up at a friend's house, asking to see proof of an adult's supervision. When I was a freshman in high school, however, although it was awkward, it was totally within reason.

Let me explain my train of thought:

As a college student, I live alone, do homework without reminders or help, and drive myself to class. Usually, I'm even on time. I pay for my own groceries, clothing, and outings. If I call my mom to ask her for something (like a ride or some extra spending money), she might say yes, but she doesn't have to. It's my responsibility to provide those things for myself now. I have the freedom of being an adult, but that freedom comes with adult responsibilities as well.

When you're a freshman in high school, your parents probably take care of those things for you. You rarely have to worry about where your next meal will come from or how you're going to complete your math homework, because you know someone is there to help you. There's no reason for you to carry the full weight of being an adult, because you're not an adult yet.

On the flip side, as a freshman, you have to accept the cons along with the pros. If you're not carrying all the responsibilities of an adult, you can't expect to have all the freedoms either. Your parents are still in charge, whether you like it or not.

This means that when your mom or dad does something embarrassing or dorky in public, you grin and bear it, because it's not your place to say "no." If they give you a curfew of 10:30 p.m. while all your friends are allowed to stay out until midnight, you may not like it, but you need to follow their rules.

You're probably groaning right now and thinking, "Are you serious? I'm not reading this book to be lectured to about listening to my parents!"

Stay calm. There is an upside to this.

The greatest benefit of being a freshman in high school is the freedom to enjoy spending time with friends and family without worrying so much about adult obligations. Sure, you may have to leave a party early once in a while, but you can enjoy every minute of it until your curfew. You have no bills to pay, no oil to change (that's part of regular auto maintenance, by the way), and no uncomfortable dress shoes to wear (to a full-time job, which will someday seriously limit your free time).

You're a kid! Revel in the lack of responsibility. Play in the mud. Eat pizza rolls. Jump for joy. Just make sure to be home before curfew.

2. Your parents probably have your best interests at heart.

As a freshman, I often forgot that the rules were there for my own good. Now that my younger brother is a senior in high school, I'm watching him go through a lot of the same things I dealt with at his age. He's constantly negotiating for more freedom, and many times, my parents give it to him.

When they don't, he sometimes comes to me to complain. Most recently, he was upset because he wasn't allowed to take an overnight trip with a friend to another state unless a parent dropped them off and picked them up.

To him, it seemed unfair that he wasn't allowed the freedom to drive himself and his friend to their hotel. At his age, I would've felt the same way. On the flip side, now that I'm a few years removed from the situation, I realize that he isn't quite ready to take a road trip like this on his own.

Until he learns a little bit more about how to handle a potential car breakdown, or whom to call if there's an accident, it's not safe for him to be driving across state lines. As an adult, I also realize that accidents cost a lot of money, which my parents would wind up paying if he had a car wreck on a trip like this.

When I was younger, my parents weren't unreasonable with me, although I might have felt differently at the time. After working through a few power struggles, usually we all realized the best way to reach a conclusion in our debate was to meet in the middle.

Recently, my parents made a deal with my brother. If a parent could drop them off at their hotel and stay in a room nearby, they could have their weekend. My brother and his friend could run around on their own. But if they needed help, a parent would be just a phone call and a short distance away.

My brother wasn't as excited as he would have been if he were going alone. He did wind up accepting the offer, though, and he had a great time with his friend during the weekend.

At the end of the trip, he even told me that after seeing the terrible traffic in the city, he was glad he hadn't tried to drive there himself. Whether he liked it or not, my parents knew best and had his best interests at heart.

Life Hack:

Something to keep in mind

As freshmen, it's easy to forget that parents' rules aren't intended to make our lives more difficult. They are meant to keep us safe. Your parents are in charge, but their main objective is to protect you.

Knowing that doesn't necessarily make obeying the rules easier or more fun, but in the long run, it helps to remember that parents have a purpose. Their end goal is to watch you grow up happy and healthy.

The next time your parents won't give you every ounce of freedom you think you deserve, take a deep breath, and let it go. Soon, you'll be old enough to make the rules for yourself. For now, though, let your parents do their job of helping you figure things out along the way.

Reflection _____ questions for freshmen

What is one rule you have to follow in your home? Is there a rule you've had to obey that really made you angry?

SOPHOMORE

Finding your place again

I asked my friend Chase, now a senior in college, to describe what he remembered about his sophomore year of high school. He responded, "I remember it was a year of trying to establish myself and figure out who I wanted to be."

That sounds about right. My sophomore year certainly was about finding my place in high school. It was different from my freshman year because I wasn't the new kid anymore. I knew my way around and had made a number of new friends, so it felt like a time to develop a bit of social grounding. I wanted a group or activity that would define me in some way and make me memorable.

That was how I found myself standing onstage in front of God and everybody, belting my lungs out at an audition for our high school's musical theatre program.

Now, fast-forward a few months, through many hours of rehearsals, to our opening night. I was feeling like a big shot. I had found my place in high school as a theatre star, and now I felt like an adult (at least for a few moments). Mission accomplished.

I soon learned that adulthood wasn't a permanent status. Not yet, anyway.

The following week, I went back to work as a cashier in a local shoe store. For the previous six months, my job had been to close the store, meaning I'd run a vacuum across the floor around 10 p.m. and head home for the night, in time for my 11 p.m. curfew. Some nights, if I was required to stay later, it was my responsibility to call home and let my parents know I would be late.

After my show, however, I felt like I was way beyond an 11 p.m. curfew, and I was sure my parents recognized that, too.

One night after work, I was in the mood for a milkshake, so I drove on over to a 24-hour fast food restaurant. I took my sweet time finishing my shake before heading home. With no phone call beforehand, I wandered into the house around midnight. What waited for me wasn't pretty.

After a long conversation (i.e., lecture) with my parents about responsibility and my still-in-effect curfew, I went to bed frustrated. How could they not recognize my maturity? Didn't they see me on stage? What was their problem?

The problem, I realize now, was that I assumed I deserved more freedom than I was ready for. Yes, I thought I deserved to stay out late, but that wasn't my decision to make.

As a sophomore in high school, you're probably looking for a little more freedom. After all, you're not a freshman anymore. It's normal and completely okay to venture a little further than last year.

My mistake wasn't in seeking a greater degree of freedom; it was that I claimed that freedom without consulting anyone. Remember, your parents are still in charge, and they have your best interests at heart. If you feel like you're ready to fly a bit further from the nest, it's still your responsibility to check in with them, to be sure you're all on the same page.

When you're asking your parents to grant you some leeway, there is one important thing to remember: Ask for exactly what you want, but be ready for them to say no.

Your parents probably have a pretty good idea of your

capabilities. It's not realistic to expect them to say "yes" to everything you suggest, and you need to be okay with that.

The key to earning greater amounts of freedom is to be willing to meet your parents in the middle, and then show them you can handle the extra freedom.

If you're looking to stay out later than usual, like I was, talk to your parents about it. If you ask for midnight and they bargain you back to 11 p.m., then accept the offer and make sure to be home by 11 p.m.

When your parents see that you can consistently handle a little more responsibility, they'll likely become even more flexible as you continue to demonstrate that you're trustworthy.

Life Hack:

Figuring out who you are

Sophomore year is a time to figure out who you are and what you are capable of. It's exciting to earn a bit more freedom as you get older, yet it's also important to appreciate and take seriously each new freedom.

Each time your parents trust you with something new, show them that you can handle it with maturity. For me, sophomore year was a year of learning about responsibility and enjoying the new freedoms that came with it.

Reflection

How have your responsibilities changed since middle school?

What freedoms do you enjoy now that were off-limits a few years ago?

JUNIOR

Pulling and pushing at the same time

Junior year comes with a lot of changes, especially in your relationship with your parents.

At this point, you may have a driver's license. A lot of juniors have jobs as well. You've probably begun thinking about life after high school. Adulthood isn't too far around the corner.

In some ways, I remember my junior year as being a time when I both pulled away from my parents and clung to them more tightly than ever before.

The day I received my driver's license, I drove my mom home afterward, feeling very proud of my accomplishment. As we pulled into the driveway, I was considering myself a full-fledged adult.

She, apparently, felt the same way, because as soon as I put the car into park, she hopped out and said, "Okay, how about running to the grocery store now to pick up some bread?"

All of a sudden, I didn't feel so grown up anymore.

Let me put this into perspective. In the state of Tennessee, it's illegal to drive by yourself until you've received a driver's license. (With a learner's permit, you can drive as long as there's at least one adult in the car.) Therefore, this would be my first time ever on the road alone.

I had never been on the interstate, or even on a busy road, by myself. The grocery store was about five minutes from our house, but as I imagined driving there alone, those few miles seemed to stretch on forever.

In the meantime, my mom was still standing next to the car, dangling the keys in front of my face, waiting for me to say something.

"I... uh... okay, I guess so."

Pulling out of the driveway and back onto the road, I felt younger than I had in years. I wanted to throw the car into park and run inside, chucking the keys out of sight and forgetting every adult responsibility I'd ever had.

As it turned out, I took a deep breath, drove five minutes down the road, bought some bread, and drove back home.

That was the first moment I realized I wasn't quite ready to be a full-fledged adult. There was a lot about growing up that frightened me, whether I wanted to admit it or not.

As a high school junior, you may feel the pace of your life picking up fairly quickly. There may be times when you wish life would slow down again. At other times, however, you may feel the opposite, like life is holding you back.

As you begin to consider life after high school, whether it's college or working full-time, the upcoming changes can feel intimidating. I've since learned that I wasn't the only one who felt intimidated. So did my mom and dad.

Now I realize it was hard for my mom to hand me her car keys and watch me drive away by myself. If she had her choice, I probably would've stuck around to keep her passenger seat warm for the next couple of years. As it was, though, she knew I was ready for a bit more responsibility, and she put me in the driver's seat, literally.

You'll probably experience a similar give-and-take of responsibility as a junior. Of course, it's easy to want greater freedom for things like staying out late with your friends, but it may seem less appealing when it comes to handling challenges, such as applying for college or networking in search of a career.

When you bargain for more freedom as a junior, don't be surprised when your parents give you some challenging responsibilities to go along with the enjoyable privileges. Part of growing up is learning to handle adult obligations.

For example, if you ask your parents to borrow the car to meet friends for dinner, they may say yes, but then also put you in charge of paying for your own gas and food while you're out. Although that may be more responsibility than you've had in the past, your parents are trying to teach you to become self-reliant.

Life Hack:

A balancing act

Junior year is all about learning to balance exciting adult freedoms with challenging responsibilities. Since you're only a couple years away from flying the coop, remember to enjoy the fun moments of your junior year and to take the difficult ones in stride as best you can.

Growing up is a challenge, but it can also be very exciting. If you find yourself overwhelmed by the responsibilities of adulthood, just remember, your parents have already been there, done that. They can help as you learn how to handle the freedoms and obligations they're giving you, and they can show you ways to make the most of your junior year.

Reflection

What are some freedoms you have now that weren't available to you when you were a freshman or sophomore?

What new responsibilities do you think you're ready for as a junior?

SENIOR

Keep your head in the game

Senior year is awesome. You're finally at the top of the heap, classes are a breeze, and freshmen look so tiny!

There's one big thing to watch out for during your last year of high school, though, and that's "senioritis." Students with senioritis suffer from symptoms such as bad moods, taking friends and family for granted, and saying things like "I just can't wait to get out of here," and "Things will be so much better after high school."

Senioritis can spoil your last year of high school. It spreads quickly, and many students succumb to it before graduation. It can ruin what should be your absolute best year of high school.

Even if most of your friends seem to have their bags packed and are headed for the door, don't forget that your life is soon going to change completely. This is your last chance to enjoy things the way they are right now.

One of my favorite high school teachers, Coach Faust, told us every week to enjoy high school, because, as he explained, it was "the last time your family and friends will all be in one place." I didn't believe it at the time, but he was right.

That's not to say you should sit around stressing about life after high school. Don't worry. It can be a lot of fun, too. My point is that you'll have plenty of time to enjoy post-high school later.

Senior year is one of your last opportunities to spend time with friends and family in a relaxed atmosphere, without too much responsibility. Even if you stay in touch later, it won't be as simple as coming home, hanging out with your family, getting together with friends on a moment's notice, and eating home-cooked meals every night. Things will be different soon, and moments like these will become far less common.

Your relationship with your parents will also continue to change during your senior year. As you get closer to the end of high school, you may feel like you've outgrown them or like you don't need them anymore. This is another symptom of senioritis.

When you have these feelings, remember that your parents have taken care of you for a number of years now. They've gone out of their way to make sure you've been happy, healthy, and safe, whether it was convenient for them or not. Just because you no longer need them to take care of you in the way they did when you were younger doesn't mean it's okay to take them for granted now.

Remember, in your parents' minds, you're still their child. It's difficult for them to watch you grow up and prepare to leave home, so take it a little easy on them. For example, if your parents want you to hang out at home and help around the house for an afternoon, stay in and oblige them now and then, even if your friends are all going out together.

It's normal (and appropriate) to feel more grown up, and you may be ready to take off and do life on your own for a while. Even so, make sure not to leave your parents in the dust. You've been the focus of their lives for many years, so even as high school graduation approaches, make sure they know how much they mean to you.

If I could redo my senior year, I'd spend more time with my family and less time on other lower-priority activities (such as working, stressing about exams, petty arguments with friends, etc.).

With friends, work, and classes, as a senior, it can feel like there's no time to stop and rest, much less to fit your family into the equation. As hard as it may seem, the key to a successful senior year is to focus on the important things and not spread yourself too thin.

So, before you erase family dinner night from your calendar, look again to see if there are other areas of your life where you might be spending a little more time than is necessary. As often as possible, make your family a priority. At the end of the year, you'll be glad you did.

Life Hack:

Days go slowly. Years go quickly.

Senior year goes by in an instant. After graduation, you'll look back and wonder where the high school years have gone.

You're going through many changes, but remember, so is your family. They are worried about life after graduation, too. Their child is becoming an adult, and family relationships are changing. That's normal, but it can still be challenging. Make an effort to make time for your family. With any luck, they'll be with you long after high school is a distant memory.

Reflection

What can you do to avoid the pitfalls of senioritis?

What changes have you seen in your family as you approach the end of high school?

All Grades

Reflection

Read Galatians 6: 7-10 (NIV)

[7] Do not be deceived: God cannot be mocked. A man reaps what he sows. [8] Whoever sows to please their flesh, from the flesh will reap destruction; whoever sows to please the Spirit, from the Spirit will reap eternal life. [9] Let us not become weary in doing good, for at the proper time we will reap a harvest if we do not give up. [10] Therefore, as we have opportunity, let us do good to all people, especially to those who belong to the family of believers.

This passage sounds a little scary at the beginning, but the focus is on how we treat each other. The writer reminds us to do good to all people. That includes parents and family members.

What can you do this year to improve the way you treat others?

It's natural to have disagreements with your parents during high school. What can you do to keep those to a minimum?

How does being a responsible family member "please the Spirit?"

What are some areas in your life you need to work on in order to improve your ability to "do good to all people?"

A Word From Zach

Allow me to get this out in the open before we go any further... Parents are sometimes right.

Let's face it — they've been in our shoes, and they know what it's like to be a teenager. If your parents seem to be "strict" or "overly-protective," it's probably because they care so much about you. I didn't learn that truth until my junior year in high school, which was about ten years too late.

When I got my driver's license at age 16, my parents made me tell them everywhere I was going before I could leave the house. Initially, I thought this was because they didn't want me to have any fun. I quickly realized, however, that most of the time, when I called my parents after a football game to ask if I could go out with friends, they would ask where I was going, give me a curfew, and let me go.

It took me several years, but I finally realized my parents weren't trying to keep me from enjoying life. They just wanted to make sure I was always safe.

As we go through high school, it's easy to feel as if our parents are still treating us like children. But, let's face it. It's almost always for our own good.

Through the Years with Ashley & Zach

Disguised as his favorite TV character at a truck stop.

Ash stars in her middle school production of *Beauty and the Beast.*

Zach and Ashley dress up for a Christmas picture.

Through the Years with Ashley & Zach

Dressed up as a hot dog and a crayon.

14-year-old Zach loved this bus!

Through the Years with Ashley & Zach

The aspiring actress takes "headshots" for her first play.

Zach fell in love with Nashville during a day trip.

Through the Years with Ashley & Zach

Ashley broke the news to her dad gently. "Dad, they're going to dye my hair dark for *Legally Blonde.*"

Zach always loved the beach!

Through the Years with Ashley & Zach

Zach plays in the snow when he was 10 years old.

11 years old

Through the Years with Ashley & Zach

First prom, with friends.

Ashley loved visiting a museum at age 14.

12-year-old Zach at a museum.

At 10, Zach loved to draw.

Through the Years with Ashley & Zach

Guess who is inside the suit.
If you guessed "Zach," you are right!

Zach and I took turns being the mascot for a local children's newspaper. The first time it was my turn, the newspaper was sponsoring an event at the zoo. It was the hottest day in our town's history, hitting 103° while I was in the costume! I had to take a break in an air-conditioned room every ten minutes.

Through the Years with Ashley & Zach

I was elected to serve on the homecoming court twice during my four years of high school. Both times, I was nominated by a service club in which I was a member.

What's Different?

Zachary loves making changes to photos. There are at least six differences between the photos below. See how many you can find.

Zach sometimes modeled for a "What's Different?" puzzle in a local children's newspaper. Little kids would sometimes recognize Zach from the puzzles when he was at the mall.

Chapter 5

Expectations vs. Reality

Primer

If you grew up watching the *High School Musical* movies, you probably expected high school to be a magical place ruled by theatre students who sing and dance through class. On the other hand, if *Mean Girls* was your unfortunate introduction to high school, you may have been afraid to show your face in the halls on your first day.

The truth is that there's a lot of hype surrounding high school. Some is good, some is bad, and a lot is inaccurate.

I asked my friends to list some ways high school defied their expectations, and here's what they had to say:

"I was expecting cliques but I never really saw them. Sure, you had theatre, band, sports, popular kids, etc., but they all pretty much intermingled with each other."

Michelle L.

"My parents told me I needed to know my social security number in high school, but I didn't believe them. Turns out, they were right!"

Emory H.

"I thought there would be a lot of drama in high school, but it wasn't like that at all."

Abby B.

"Teachers in middle school made high school sound scary; then high school teachers made college sound scary. High school and college are both a lot of work, but each one has been better than the one before it."

Ariel F.

"I thought there would be a popular clique that completely ran the school. There were a few people everyone knew, but I never saw anyone fear them or anything."

Virginia C.

"I thought prom would be the most important night of my life and that it was crucial to have a date. Actually, I had an amazing time going to prom with my friends, and I've had a lot of fun, meaningful nights since then, too."

Elena M.

"I thought it would be hard to make friends. Movies make it seem like high school is that way, but it wound up being pretty easy."

Chase B.

"I thought I would have too many classes and wouldn't be able to keep up. In reality, I figured it out and learned a lot in the process."

Kayla J.

"I thought there would be crazy parties all the time, like in the movies, but I actually don't know anybody who ever went to one."

Vanessa S.

What expectations did you (or do you) have before beginning high school?

If you were to write a list of things that have turned out differently than you expected over the last year or two, what would be on that list?

FRESHMAN

High School is nothing like TV

My biggest high school surprise came in my freshman year, during the first week of classes. Having grown up in a tight-knit middle school community, I expected high schoolers to be monsters.

Some of my teachers had made high school out to sound like an impossible task, telling us the teachers taught much faster, refusing to go back and explain confusing subjects.

Also, I was sure the lunchroom would be separated into obvious cliques and that I would stick out like a sore thumb. I wasn't athletic, my hair was still its natural color, and I didn't carry a skateboard or an art palette with me. Clearly, I would be an outcast without some physical characteristic that assigned me to a particular group.

Even worse, I was terrified of upperclassmen. I'd heard horror stories about freshmen being packed into lockers or thrown into trash cans, and as a result, I was determined not to be noticed on the first day of school.

In reality, high school was nothing like I'd seen on television or in the movies. There weren't any rivalries between the cheerleaders and the choir students like I'd seen in *Glee,* or any dangerously-cute boys ready to fall head over heels in love with me like in *Ten Things I Hate About You.*

To be honest, the first day of high school was, well, pretty uneventful.

To ease your worries about freshman year, allow me to dispel some common high school myths right away:

- Regardless of what you might have heard, teachers are (generally) nice and helpful.

- The lunchroom is a big hodge-podge of students sitting in random groups throughout the room, and it's not too hard to grab an empty seat.

- Upperclassmen aren't interested in underclassmen for the most part, and they often don't even share any classes with them.

- It is highly unlikely someone will fall in love with you on the first day. All the other students are too busy worrying about finding their classes and getting adjusted to a new school year, just like you are.

Something else that surprised me in high school was learning that not everyone was a Christian. If you grew up in a relatively small, heavily-religious community like I did, it might seem like Christianity is the one common denominator everyone shares. Not so in high school.

I experienced a bit of culture shock when I found out that several of my best friends were either agnostic (being unsure if there's a god or not) or atheist (believing with certainty that there is no god). It shook me even more when I realized that these people weren't at all how I had imagined non-religious people to be.

They didn't cuss all the time or participate in illicit activities. They didn't drink or do drugs, and they weren't partiers. Most of them were smart, kind, and funny, and it really threw me for a loop.

In reality, I learned that not everyone is a Christian, and that doesn't mean others are going to be awful or scary. I learned a lot from my non-Christian friends, and I found I could openly discuss religion with most of them.

At the end of the day, my church community became much more important to me in high school. It's fantastic to meet all kinds of people at school and make new friends regardless of anyone's religion, but that means you'll need your church community to help keep you grounded. For me, church actually served as a great sounding board for many of the hard questions I had throughout my freshman year.

Although many of my high school friends didn't fit into my preconceived notions, I learned as a freshman that my experience wasn't totally isolated. At church, I found out that many of my youth group friends felt the same way about school, and we had the chance to talk to youth leaders and adults who had already gone through this process, when they had experienced similar feelings years before.

I grew a lot in high school. I asked a lot of tough questions, knowing that my church was a home base I could always count on. No matter how much I wondered or struggled, there were people there who knew more than I did and were willing to help me think things through.

When it was all said and done, I felt more secure in my faith than ever before. I realize now that thinking more deeply forced me to decide why I believe what I believe and helped me to establish legitimate grounding for my faith.

Life Hack:

Face your challenges

I hope you experience similar challenges and opportunities throughout high school. Inevitably, some of the changes will be tough, but with courage and determination, you will be able to face them head on, and in the end, you'll be so glad you did.

Reflection questions for freshmen

How do you feel when you meet someone who is different than you?

What adult can you trust and turn to when you have questions about your life?

SOPHOMORE

Don't let stress get the best of you

As I've explained before, sophomore year is an exciting time in high school. You're not a freshman anymore, so school doesn't seem as big or intimidating as it did last year. You probably have a few friends by now, and you're beginning to establish your place in the school.

As a sophomore, I was so busy finding my place and creating my reputation that sometimes it felt like who I was in high school would determine who I would be for the rest of my life. I frequently stayed up late, stressing about making perfect grades, finding a great job, and never missing a football game.

For that reason, sophomore superlatives were a turning point for me. When the list came out and I realized I'd been nominated for an award, I was seriously excited. People had noticed me! If I won a superlative, I would earn my own page in the yearbook. That seemed like a dream come true.

Superlative winners were announced at the end of the school talent show every year, and I rolled into the auditorium that day feeling confident. After all, I had as good a chance as anyone, right?

After the talent show, I found my friends, and we sat together, anxiously awaiting the awards ceremony. A few minutes later, the principal began. First, he announced the winner for "Most Talented." That wasn't me. Actually, one of my friends from choir soon jogged up the steps to the stage, excitedly accepting the award. I dutifully applauded, trying to ignore the twinge of jealousy in my stomach.

It's okay, I told myself. Surely, my turn was coming. A few more categories were announced, and I remember thinking *Maybe I'll be next.*

Finally, there was only one category left, my category: "Best All-Around." At that point, the principal called all of the nominees to the stage. I tried to stay confident as I stood there, surrounded by four or five other students who were each well-known and well-liked.

Holding the winner card in his hand, the principal quieted the crowd. I felt the butterflies in my stomach go crazy.

"The winner in the "Best All-Around" category is..."

He shouted the winning name to the cheering crowd.

It wasn't my name.

Slowly, I trudged back to my seat. I was welcomed by my friends, who all patted my back, told me I'd done a great job, and reminded me that being nominated was an honor in itself. Sure, I thought, that's easy for you to say. Nevertheless, I forced a half-smile and pretended to be grateful for the nomination.

In the days following the award ceremony, I walked around the school in a haze, trying to re-establish the confident, excited feeling I'd had just a few days before.

You're one of the most talented people in the school, I told myself in choir. But I was quickly rebutted by the memory of not winning a superlative award in that category.

You're one of the friendliest people in the school, I said to myself as I ate lunch with a group of friends. But I felt my heart sink when I remembered that I hadn't won "Friendliest."

That weekend, I went to youth group at church, and one of my favorite counselors picked up on my moodiness. He pulled me aside to ask what was wrong, and I told him that I just wasn't sure how to find my place. What was I doing wrong to not win an award?

He sat down with me right then and told me that he had been nominated for a superlative in high school himself.

"Really? What was it?" I asked, surprised – mostly because it was hard to picture my youth counselor as ever having been in high school.

He laughed. "To be honest, I don't even remember! Things like that stop mattering so much after high school. Eventually, you realize that no matter how good you are at something, there will always be others who are equally good, or even better."

I didn't understand why he was laughing. It sounded awfully defeating to me, and I asked him what the point of trying was, if he already knew he'd never be the best. His response has stuck with me, and I still remember it when I face situations where I'm striving too hard for perfection.

"Well," he told me, "I think true value comes from finding joy in the things you're doing, as well as feeling good about a job well done, whether you win or lose. People who do things well and with a good attitude often stand out even more than those who are technically 'the best.'"

I had never thought about it that way. When I returned to school the following week, I tried to focus less on receiving recognition from others and more on finding joy in the feeling of a job well done.

Since my sophomore year of high school, I've changed a lot, but my youth counselor's advice is still true. No matter how many classes I take, extracurricular activities I sign up for, or jobs I master, someone will always be a little bit better.

That doesn't matter nearly as much to me now, though, because my experience of focusing on the internal reward of doing good work with a good attitude has served me so much better than striving for perfection ever did.

Life Hack:

Find satisfaction along the way

Today, I'm working on forging my own path, in my college classes and in a job I really enjoy. When I receive compliments on my work ethic or my attitude, it's much more meaningful than being recognized once for being "the best."

So, you may or may not win a high school superlative. You might find the perfect niche or activity and be the best at what you do, or you may not. Either way, the world keeps turning.

Ultimately, as a sophomore, just focus on enjoying whatever you choose to do. Find satisfaction in being a great worker, friend, family member, or student. In the long run, nobody remembers who was voted "Best All-Around" in high school, but your friends and family will always remember the positive impact you made on their lives.

Reflection

If you could win any superlative award, which award would you choose for yourself?

How important to you is winning? Would you call yourself a good loser or a bad loser?

JUNIOR

Great Expectations

As I approached my junior year, I had big expectations about two things: prom and standardized testing.

The Truth About Prom:

In my thinking, prom would be just like the ones I'd seen in the movies. Sure, I only had a couple of guy friends, most of whom I'd known since elementary school, but that didn't deter me.

Wasn't it a given that a few weeks before prom I'd fall in love with some handsome, mysterious stranger who had transferred into my high school just in time for the dance? That was always what happened in the chick flicks.

In reality, a few months before the dance, a boy did ask me out. It seemed too good to be true – maybe this was the chick flick moment I'd been waiting for. It took me a second to respond, because in my head, I was running through all the prom adventures we would have. He would pick me up at my house in a limo, or maybe a horse-drawn carriage. I would float down the stairs in my ball gown. Well, you know the story.

"Ashley? Are you okay?" I remember him saying. "I asked if you were planning to go to prom."

"Oh, I don't know," I answered shyly. "I mean, I was thinking about it. What about you?"

I spoke the truth, as I had thought about prom pretty much every day since I began high school. His reply, however, snapped me back into reality a little too quickly.

"No, I don't think so," he continued. "I went last year with my older sister's friend. It was sort of lame. I mean, unless you really want to go or something."

"I guess you're right," I stuttered. "That's okay."

"Okay, cool," he told me. "I figured you wouldn't really want to go, but I just thought I'd mention it. I'll see you later."

With that, my fantasies were shattered. I was left in a junior girl's nightmare scenario: dateless, with only a few weeks before prom.

Thankfully, my mom (as usual) knew just what to do. I came home in tears because of the prom date fiasco, and she taught me one of the most important lessons I will ever learn: Life can be good, even incredibly fun, without a prom date or a significant other.

That afternoon, Mom told me to hop in the car because we were going for a drive. Although I was confused and still upset, I did as I was told. Ten minutes later, we pulled into the mall parking lot. I followed my mom up the stairs and into the dress department of JCPenney.

Immediately, I recoiled, unwilling to walk through the groups of girls who were there with their parents and friends, giggling while they prepared for prom. Mom pulled me through the crowd anyway, though, and picked out five or six dresses for me to try on.

After putting on the first couple of gowns, my tears subsided, and I even started to smile. Twirling around the dressing room, I felt like a princess, with or without a prom date.

By that evening, I had picked out the perfect dress. (As a bonus, it was only $30. I found it on the clearance rack, and it fit perfectly.) I messaged 10 of my girlfriends about getting a group together to go to the dance. Amazingly, none of them had been invited by a boy either, and all of them said yes to my suggestion.

On the night of prom, my girlfriends and I showed up looking fancy and had the time of our lives taking pictures and laughing together. We went out for a nice dinner beforehand, and I ordered chicken tenders off the kids' menu, totally comfortable chowing down in a prom dress in front of my friends.

We spent most of the evening running around as a big group, and we had a great time at the dance. The next day, my "almost prom date" told me he'd seen pictures of me with my friends before prom, and he felt like he missed out. I smiled and said it would have been fun with him, but secretly, I knew I'd had twice as much fun going with my friends.

As you think about prom, remember that junior year can feel intimidating and overwhelming anyway, as many people earn their drivers' licenses and begin to date more seriously. I learned that whether you choose to date or not, your life has incredible potential to be fun and exciting. Several of my college friends stayed single throughout high school, and most of them say they are better for it. They're confident young adults who know how to enjoy life, even when they're not attached to someone else.

To those who do choose to date in high school, one of the best pieces of advice I can give you is to continue to spend time with your friends and family. Dating in high school is normally short-term; significant others tend to come and go. It's easy to be infatuated in the moment, but in the long run, your friends and family are the ones who will stick around. Don't take them for granted.

At prom time, if you find yourself date-less like I did, it's not the end of the world. Life will go on, and you can have as much (or even more) fun enjoying your time with friends and family.

Prom is just one night of your life, and it probably won't even be one of the nights you most remember once you become an adult. So, don't sweat the small stuff. Whether you attend prom or not, enjoy the moments that make up high school, and remember: You can look forward to many more special times to come.

The Truth About Grades and Standardized Testing

As a high school student, I spent a lot of time worrying about my grades. My schedule was filled with honors classes, and I worked hard to stay in good graces with my teachers throughout my junior year.

A couple of months into my junior year, one of my teachers handed out thick packets of information about upcoming standardized exams. I felt my heart drop into my stomach when the teacher explained that the ACT would partially determine whether or not we made it into college, as well as how much scholarship money we would receive. (Many high schools also offer the SAT, an equivalent exam.)

Needless to say, that's a lot of pressure for a 16-year-old.

Having taken the ACT three times, and improving my score significantly between my first and third exams, there are two important things I learned about grades and standardized exams that I want to share with you:

1. Yes, it's important to study, but...

2. Your grades do not define your value as a person.

Now, those statements may seem somewhat contradictory, so let me explain.

Standardized exams are quite difficult, like many high school exams. They are designed that way. You aren't going to be able to answer every question perfectly, and you probably aren't going to score in the top percentile on your first try.

Many students fall into the trap of thinking they aren't smart or worthwhile because they don't make good grades or score well on standardized exams. In truth, your actual score doesn't matter nearly as much as you think it does.

What matters is your work ethic and the effort you put forth to improve.

As I mentioned, I took the ACT three times, each time scoring higher than I had on the previous test. Although I never made a perfect score on any of the exams, I did learn that some study tactics helped me more than others. I was able to identify the learning tools that were most effective for me. When college admissions advisors looked at my scores, they didn't consider the end result nearly as much as they observed my overall level of improvement and my ability to learn.

By the way, this is true in many areas of life, not just in standardized testing.

One of my classmates scored one point away from perfect on the ACT. Instead of focusing on his extraordinary achievement, however, he was very upset about missing that final point. I've learned that if you hold yourself to a standard of perfection, you will always be disappointed in yourself. It doesn't matter how smart or incredible you are, you are human. You will make mistakes.

One person who has taught me a lot about learning from failure is my boss. She hired me when I was only a junior in college, brand new to corporate office work. In the months I've worked with her, she has shown me how to face challenges with a positive attitude and make the most of my opportunities. I owe a lot to her.

So, wherever you find yourself during high school, it's important to approach your school work with a positive attitude. You won't ever be perfect, but you will improve over time. Just put in the hours and the effort, and cut yourself some slack now and then.

Life Hack:

Find satisfaction along the way

Junior year is the perfect time to practice focusing on improvement rather than perfection. With college just around the corner, you're sure to have some exciting challenges ahead, and then, with a little effort, you'll be able to handle almost anything life throws your way.

Reflection _____ questions for juniors

Have you felt a lot of pressure about standardized tests?

What is one thing you can do to make your junior year less stressful and more fun?

SENIOR

Life after high school

Senior year is a biggie! It's your last year of high school, so it's a great time to catch up with lots of different friends before you pack up and take off on your next big adventure. Senior year also comes with a lot of changes, as you prepare to head out into the world of adulthood.

One major misconception I had as a senior was that life after high school would look the same for me. I expected that I would have the same friends, participate in the same activities (choir nerd for life!), and still spend evenings at home with my family every week.

Although things did stay the same in some areas, I was wrong about adulthood feeling just like high school. Slowly, bits and pieces of my life changed as adulthood came into sharper focus.

On college move-in day, my family, my best friend, and I moved everything into my dorm room and spent the afternoon setting it up. Our door squeaked, the window didn't open, we were missing pieces of a bed frame, and a family of mice had built their home in one corner of the room. Although I was excited, by the end of the day I was also completely overwhelmed by the drastic change that was about to become my "new normal" for the next four years.

After we finished putting the room together, my parents hugged me goodbye and drove away. I was left standing there with my friend, at a complete loss for what to do next.

We spent the evening running around campus, trying to

get our bearings and figuring out what in the world to do. We met lots of new people and participated in some of the activities for new students on campus. Around midnight, I excused myself and wandered back to my dorm, feeling proud of myself for having survived the first day on campus.

As soon as I crawled into my bed, though, I started to cry.

Now I realize how dumb I probably looked, sitting in a dorm bed and crying to a family of mice in the corner while all my friends were just down the hall. That wasn't what I expected my first day of college to look like. The point is, though, I survived. And after a week or two, I was thriving.

You have those transitions to look forward to, but right now, just enjoy your senior year to the fullest, and take advantage of the spontaneous friend gatherings and the opportunities to spend evenings with your family. These moments are precious and short-lived. Although the future will be exciting, the present won't be like this for much longer.

The reality of senior year is that you're at the top of the food chain, living it up in your last year of high school. That's exactly what you're supposed to be doing. You've waited a long time for this year. Now, it's your turn!

On the flip side, remember that life will continue beyond high school. After graduation, you and your friends will move on to the next stage of life, whatever that may be. There will be some challenging days, along with some fun days, as you transition from high school into adulthood. Chances are that you will survive, and, hopefully, you will learn to thrive, too.

Life Hack:

Enjoy your senior year

Your adventure after graduation will look different than it did during high school, but that doesn't mean it will be any less exciting. You're growing toward adulthood, after all. You wouldn't want to stay in high school forever. I promise.

For now, try to really enjoy your senior year. Don't get caught up in senioritis and spend too much time focusing on what happens next. Life will never be quite like this again, so appreciate each moment as it comes. Buckle down and determine what you need to do now to prepare for life after high school, but remember to live fully in the present.

Senior year is what you've been waiting for, after all. Make the most of it!

Reflection

Now that you're a senior, how has your outlook on life changed since your freshman year?

How do you think you might change during your upcoming college years?

On a scale of 1 (not stressed at all) to 10 (totally stressed), how are you feeling about the end of your high school career?

All Grades

Reflection questions for everyone

Read Matthew 6:34 (NIV)

[34] "Therefore do not worry about tomorrow, for tomorrow will worry about itself. Each day has enough trouble of its own."

What are some troubles you have recently faced?

Is there anything about the future that sometimes causes you to worry?

What are some steps you could take to avoid dwelling on the future?

A Word From
Zach

My sister is right. High school is nothing like what you see in the movies or on TV. There are no musical numbers, the football players are not mean to all the "nerds," and the lunch room is not a labyrinth of cliques. High school is just a place where a bunch of kids are learning to fit in and trying to have some fun at the same time. So, if you like socializing, get some friends together. If you like music, join the band or the choir. If you like studying, invite some other smart people over to hit the books with you after school.

Here's an overall summary of what to expect in high school: You'll have some great teachers and some not-so-great teachers; you'll make some fantastic friends and maybe run into a few people you don't like so much. Regardless of what you see in the movies, plan on your experience being something unique and special to you.

Honestly, I've loved almost every minute of high school.

Chapter 6

Holding Onto My Faith
Through All This

Primer

On my first day of college, I entered my Intro to Communications class to find one word scrawled on the whiteboard in giant letters:

CHANGE

My professor introduced herself to the class and asked, "Why do you think I wrote this up here?"

Several students guessed it was because the first day of college brought lots of change or because our lives were about to change significantly in the next four years.

"That word is on the board," she explained, "because I want you all to remember for the rest of your college careers, and the rest of your lives, that change is one of the only constants you will ever encounter in life."

What? I wasn't sure what she meant, but I realized that my first college class might already be going deeper than I was prepared for.

"Yes, your lives will change in college, but the changes don't begin or end there," she continued. "When you were young children, you started kindergarten. That was a big change at the time. After that came first grade and then second grade, each different than the one before. Now, you're experiencing college, another big change, and after you graduate, don't you think your lives will change again?"

The class nodded in agreement. We were beginning to understand.

The teacher transitioned into a lecture about how change would impact our professional lives and how we had to be ready to roll with the punches. As far as I was concerned, however, the most important lesson had already been taught. Change is a constant we can always count on.

This is true of our spiritual lives as well.

Goodness knows, my personal faith has changed significantly since middle and high school, and it will continue to evolve as I transition into post-grad life.

At first, the thought of a changing faith was terrifying, but I understand that change is good and even necessary. There are times we need to wrestle with hard questions, even if it means questioning why we believe what we believe. If you are like me, you will find yourself a better person for understanding the foundation of your beliefs and your faith.

Through my personal search, I learned several valuable lessons. One of the most important was understanding that, at the end of the day, I serve a God who is constant.

The Bible is replete with verses about God's faithful, unchanging nature.

Jesus Christ is the same yesterday and today and forever.
Hebrews 13:8 (NIV)

Even to your old age and gray hairs, I am He, I am He who will sustain you. I have made you and I will carry you. I will sustain you and I will rescue you.
Isaiah 46:4 (NIV)

Just as I did, you may soon find yourself asking some hard questions.

How does knowing that you serve a God who is
faithful and unchanging affect your life as a high
school student?

FRESHMAN

Taking your faith for granted

As a freshman, you may be painfully aware that
change is a constant in your life right now. Whether you're
headed into high school with ten friends or none, your experience is guaranteed to be different than it was last year in
middle school. High school is an environment in which it's not
unusual to start experiencing challenges and changes related
to your faith.

For me, changes in my faith seemed minimal compared
to everything else that was happening during my freshman
year. I was in a new building with new teachers and different students, and I had no idea who to talk to or how to find
my way around. Needless to say, deepening my spiritual life
wasn't exactly my number one priority on my first day of
high school.

Throughout the first year, in fact, my personal faith didn't
change noticeably, since my parents still called the shots for
the most part. Whether I liked it or not, we were up on Sunday
mornings to go to Sunday school and church, then off to a

106

Mexican restaurant for lunch. Despite changes at school, I was still surrounded by the same youth group friends I'd known in elementary and middle school, and the pastors and counselors were familiar faces, too.

Looking back, I realize I often took my church community for granted as a freshman. I've now come to realize that in the midst of so much change, church was actually one of the few things that seemed to stay the same. Even though waking up early was always a struggle, that normalcy was what I needed, and it prepared me to ride the wave of family and school challenges that I would face throughout the year.

Whether you're about to start high school or you're already there, your life will probably feel hectic sometimes, and that's when it's important to lean on your faith. During the crazy times, it's nice to know you can always count on a God who is unchanging, as well as a community of believers that has been around for centuries.

On the flip side, many of my friends experienced drastic changes in their faith during freshman year. Some who had been members of the youth group for years suddenly stopped showing up for events. Also, a few students who had never been regulars started coming more often, and new people began showing up for youth group meetings as well.

Why the drastic change in attendance? I realize now that high school is a time of exposure to new ideas and concepts, and many students begin to wrestle with tough questions about their faith. Some dive in, realizing this is the chance to really grow deeper and learn more about their faith, while others go in the opposite direction, pulling away from church activities.

A few of my middle school friends began visiting different churches during high school. Some of them didn't find what they were looking for, but others found church communities that really seemed to help them grow in their faith.

My advice to a high school freshman wrestling with tough faith questions during an ever-changing time in life is to hang on to the faith that has brought you this far. For one thing, the best place to bring your tough questions is to a group of people who have had similar experiences in their lives. Yes, it's intimidating and can even be downright frightening at times, but after asking tough questions for several years now, I realize that God isn't intimidated by our questions or deep thinking.

Life Hack:

A time of change

Will you always find the answer you're looking for? Not necessarily.

There are some questions that have been asked continually for centuries. That's probably because they're too difficult to answer during one Sunday School class or youth group meeting. If you stick with it, though, you'll likely begin to grasp more than you imagined you would. You'll begin to understand more deeply why you believe what you believe.

If you're in a church that doesn't feel right to you, maybe this year is your chance to find a new place that feels more like home. Or, maybe you are being called to stay put and step up to discuss these issues with members of your faith community. Freshman year is a time of change, and often that means taking on more responsibility.

In short, whether or not your faith changes significantly during your freshman year, it's a great time to dig into your questions and learn more about yourself and your beliefs. It may require some bravery, but remember, there is comfort in serving a God who never changes.

Reflection _____ questions for freshmen

Now that middle school is over, do you feel that any changes are taking place in the way you think or act?

If you could ask a trusted adult anything about God or your faith, what would you ask?

SOPHOMORE

Challenge yourself to grow

In previous chapters, I've described sophomore year as a time of normalizing. You're a little more familiar with your friends, your school, and your teachers. Hopefully, you've come to a new understanding with your family as well. Now that some of the changes from freshman year have become routine, it's time to enjoy a breather in many areas of your life.

Your faith, however, is not one of those areas. In fact, as your life relaxes in some ways during sophomore year, it could be the perfect time to challenge yourself to grow and learn more about your faith and what you believe.

If you already have a church or other community where you share your faith with others, that's great! If you don't have a church or youth group, this is the perfect opportunity to find a group or a place that really suits you.

Sophomore year was a great year for me in terms of my faith. I had really grown into my church's youth group and was close with the counselors and several students my age. I was learning more about my faith as well as asking big questions. It was a year of discovering what I really valued about my church community and of looking forward to attending events and going to Sunday school.

It's important to not take these moments for granted. Instead, take stock of what you're learning, identify what's working in your faith journey, and be intentional about finding new ways to grow.

Without the stress that came with being a freshman, I was more comfortable taking risks and asking important questions about my faith. At times, it was a little frightening to ask questions that might have challenged what I had always believed. But as I grew older, I began to realize I didn't need to stay at my elementary-age understanding of faith.

On the flip side, it was often difficult to translate the spiritual growth I was experiencing at church into my secular friendships at school. There's something about believing in God, or in anything important, that's hard to explain to someone who hasn't experienced it. It's like trying to describe a best friend to someone who has moved a lot and never had close friends.

That person might be happy for you, but he or she doesn't quite grasp how special a particular friendship is to you. When it comes to your faith, it can feel isolating, even frustrating, to be surrounded by people who don't understand something that is so important to you. Sophomore year was the first time in my life I had to learn how to share this huge part of who I was with friends who really didn't get it and even with some who actively resisted it.

After several slip-ups and awkward moments, I finally began to figure out how to be a Christian in a school where I wasn't always in the majority. So what do you do when you encounter a friend who isn't a Christian, when being a follower of Christ is such a fundamental part of who you are?

After a while, I learned not to offer unsolicited advice. People will be much more likely to engage in conversation when they realize it's just that – conversation. Nobody wants to be attacked on the premise that he or she is wrong. Regardless of whether or not someone shares your beliefs, it's not your job to bully or harass them into agreeing with you.

Secondly, it's important to know why you believe what you believe. It doesn't have to be perfect, but it's important to have a well-thought-out response when someone asks "Why are you a Christian?"

The first time I was asked that question, it threw me for a loop. I was the president of my youth group, so I figured I must be pretty solid in my faith, right? When I was put on the spot, however, and realized the answer was "Because my parents raised me that way," a little tingle in the back of my head told me it was time to take a more personal look into what I believed.

If you're like I was, and you don't have a solid handle on your faith as a sophomore, don't despair. The third most important thing I learned about talking to friends about faith is that it's important to be honest.

I didn't have all the answers then, and there's a good chance you don't either. If you go crashing into a conversation in a judgmental, "let-me-save-your-soul" kind of way, you risk alienating those whom you are trying to help.

On the other hand, if you're willing to admit that you don't know everything, but you'll be glad to share what you do know, that's another story. None of my friends who became Christians in high school or college did so because of a single conversation or because someone promised them all the answers. For many of them, it was the continual reminder that someone loves them unconditionally; then, eventually, they decided to accept that love without knowing all the answers.

This is how I've learned to present my faith to friends, realizing that people don't always accept it overnight. Sometimes they never accept it at all. When a conversation naturally leads in that direction, or when I'm asked, I share the basic reasons I've chosen to be a Christian. I let them know I don't have perfect answers for everything, but I'm glad to share my thoughts on anything they may have questions about. My faith is an open book, and I'm always willing to share. Then, I listen.

Often, my friends want to ask more questions or tell me what they think about what I've said, and I let them talk. It can feel awkward to talk about your faith at first, but when it becomes a conversation rather than a steamroller elevator speech, a faith talk can become quite natural and interesting.

Life Hack:

Don't shy away from your faith

It's okay to share your faith with your secular friends in high school. It's also okay to listen to them in order to learn why your non-Christian friends believe what they believe. You'll probably have more big questions following conversations like those, and that's one reason why it's so important to remain part of a faith-based organization where you can ask big questions. Don't shy away from your faith during high school simply because there are times when it's hard to understand it completely.

As Ms. Frizzle used to say on *The Magic School Bus,* the point is to "Ask questions, make mistakes, and get messy!"

This is what high school is for. Sure, it may be awkward at times, but that's part of the learning process. Time to go figure it out!

Reflection

Do you feel like you're growing closer to or moving away from God this year?

What are two or three reasons why you have hung on to your faith?

JUNIOR

Watch out for faith burnout

Junior year is when I began to experience burn-out for the first time. The high point of my sophomore year had been serving as president of my church youth group. This had meant spending three or four nights every week involved in faith-based activities.

Many of my friends, however, were now moving to other churches or youth groups or were showing up to church activities less frequently as life became increasingly busy. Youth group became a lonely place for me, as one of the remaining upperclassmen. As the president, I was still obligated to lead weekly activities and help out whenever possible, but I began seeing the group as a chore instead of a blessing.

Burnout is something many high schoolers experience. You can feel it in school, at work, and even in your faith. Thankfully, it is fixable.

I was burned out for a couple of reasons. The first was that I had outgrown my youth group. That's not to say the group was bad in any way, but as many of my friends drifted away from church activities, I had to make a firm decision to continue holding onto my faith.

Secondly, I was holding myself to an impossibly high standard. As the president of my youth group, I felt like it was my job to take care of everyone else, without any concern for my own spiritual well-being. I was shouldering a lot of big questions, giving advice, and providing a listening ear and a shoulder to cry on, but I wasn't taking enough responsibility for my own faith. After a while, I was spending so much energy worrying about my friends connecting with God that I was neglecting my own relationship with God.

As a Christian, it's so easy to focus on the "Go and make disciples" portion of the Bible and forget the "Be still and know that I am God" part.

As I mentioned earlier, however, burnout is fixable.

Life Hack:

Guard your faith

Burnout is something many high school students experience as they begin searching for more meaning in their lives. As I said, it took me a while to figure everything out, but after about a year, things began to click.

For my senior year, I decided not to run for a youth group office so I could just enjoy being a participant for a change. I took time to de-stress and to redevelop my relationship with God. It took a while, but I finally relinquished the idea that I could somehow become the "perfect Christian" by working hard enough.

Eventually, I began asking bigger questions as well as visiting churches closer to the university I would soon attend. By the time I began college, I had found a new church that was a good fit for me. Through my experience there, I began to learn even more about my faith journey.

It wasn't easy to step away from the safety net of a familiar church, but it was necessary if I wanted to continue learning and growing. Sometimes – often – growing in your faith requires leaving your comfort zone.

If you're able to hang tough and find your own place within a faith community, chances are you will learn more about God and yourself, and you'll be amazed by what you discover.

Reflection _____ questions for juniors

If you could ask God any question, what would it be?

As you grow closer to adulthood, what is something you can do to keep from becoming burned out and moving further from your faith?

SENIOR

Life after high school

If you're not already sitting (or lying) down, take a seat. What I'm about to say might shock you.

Senior year was the first time I found myself actively avoiding church. Following some burnout during my junior year, I was in a downward spiral, feeling out of place in youth group and angry when my parents pushed me to stay active in church activities. I just wanted to be done wrestling with the big questions. I was over it.

After a couple months of not attending youth group, however, I realized something strange. I wasn't particularly missing the silly games we played on Sunday and Wednesday nights, but I was craving time with other youth. Also, I missed feeling like I was a part of something bigger than myself.

I could feel the anger, hurt, and resentment of burnout falling away when I chose to read the Bible on my own. Despite my hesitance to take part in the activities I had once found so meaningful, some part of me refused to let go of the idea of God entirely. During my senior year, when I was tempted to pull back from my faith, I found myself face to face with the truth. I could run from church as far as I wanted to, but no matter how hard I tried, I couldn't run from God.

The story of Jonah resonated with me that year, remembering how he ran from God, only to learn God was with him wherever he went.

After high school graduation, I soon found myself wandering into the campus ministry center at my university for the first time. The building was full of students about my age who greeted me warmly and ushered the freshmen upstairs to the sanctuary for church. I wasn't sure what to expect, but already the environment felt different from my youth group. I was getting older, and I was ready for the change.

I liked being in a group of students closer to my age, where people were ready to dive into more challenging discussions. It was also nice to be part of a church completely by choice, knowing my parents weren't making me go. For several reasons, the campus ministry clicked for me, and I realized I'd found the right church.

Over the next few months, I learned how to discern what I liked and didn't like about my new church environment, and I began to understand what was most important for me. For example, I was happy that the sermons were geared toward college students, for the most part, and that the environment was designed to fit within our busy schedules. On the other hand, I sometimes missed seeing children and older people at church, and I realized that I'd love to find a more diverse group after graduation.

In the end, I learned that no church is perfect, and eventually I decided to give my home church one more chance. Being part of a different group had provided some much-needed perspective. Just because my home church wasn't the perfect fit for me didn't mean it wasn't a great fit for my parents or for my little brother. A diversity of churches is a wonderful thing, giving everyone the opportunity to find the place where they can best grow into their faith.

I also learned that although I had outgrown my youth group, that didn't mean I had outgrown my faith. There would be other groups. The only constant is change, after all, and one of the biggest years of change for me was my senior year in high school.

Life Hack:

Preparing for the next stage of life

My senior year was a time of experiencing full-blown burnout and learning how to recover. It was a chance to discover what was important to me in life and in a church. It was also a time in which I began to allow myself to change.

You may have similar feelings as a senior as you prepare to move on to the next stage of life. Just remember that life changes don't require abandoning the good things that have brought you this far. It's easy to "put off" faith during your senior year of high school, but it's probably a better decision to stretch and find new ways to grow in your faith.

No church, and no Christian, is perfect. That's no reason to give up your faith entirely. As you enter the first stage of adulthood, take time to understand what you really believe and become involved in activities that help you grow stronger in your faith.

Reflection

Have you ever felt like you had outgrown some of the church activities you were involved in during your younger years?

As you draw closer to high school graduation, what are some things you can do to stay connected to a faith community in the coming years?

All Grades

Reflection

Read Mark 4:35-41 (NIV)

[35] That day when evening came, he said to his disciples, "Let us go over to the other side." [36] Leaving the crowd behind, they took him along, just as he was, in the boat. There were also other boats with him. [37] A furious squall came up, and the waves broke over the boat, so that it was nearly swamped. [38] Jesus was in the stern, sleeping on a cushion. The disciples woke him and said to him, "Teacher, don't you care if we drown?"

[39] He got up, rebuked the wind and said to the waves, "Quiet! Be still!" Then the wind died down and it was completely calm.

[40] He said to his disciples, "Why are you so afraid? Do you still have no faith?"

[41] They were terrified and asked each other, "Who is this? Even the wind and the waves obey him!"

Have you ever been awakened from sleep by a hard storm?

How do you suppose Jesus was able to sleep through such a terrifying storm?

A Word From
Zach

Keeping a consistent faith in high school is a challenge for a lot of Christian teens. I was blessed with a group of friends at church that included eight other kids whom I had grown up with. Frequently, it seemed like we were all going through the same things at the same time.

Because some of my friends outside of church aren't Christians, I've often turned to my church friends when I was facing a difficult issue. Also, I've gotten a lot of advice and encouragement at church over the years from Christian mentors who are older than I am.

Over the past year, I've met with one of my pastors a few times at a restaurant, just to ask questions about my faith. Through those meetings, not only did he help me discover answers to my faith questions, he also became a good friend.

Without the support of my Christian friends and mentors at church, I don't think my faith would have grown as strongly as it has during high school.

You can read more about surviving high school by following Ashley on Facebook.

Chapter 7

The Disconnect

Primer

Last week, I watched a TED Talk video entitled "I'm Seventeen," and, to be honest, I didn't expect much. The speaker was only seventeen, after all. How much could she have to say?

I quickly realized the presenter was a high school senior with quite a bit of insight into the world. She talked about politics, education, and several hot-button issues. Then she wrapped it up with a point about how a lot of people find it easy to ignore her ideas simply because she's seventeen.

I was taken aback by her speech, realizing that I, too, had been ready to invalidate her from the beginning, based solely on her age.

The talk made me think back to high school, and I remembered how hard I'd pushed to be heard at times. It was defeating to hear adults tell me "You aren't quite old enough to understand" or "Your generation just doesn't get it." This is the reality high schoolers face every day.

In the same way, some adults seem to think life in high school is incredibly easy. After all, you aren't an adult yet. You don't pay bills or work full-time. Adults sometimes forget that high school can truly be difficult.

Whether it's family conflict, bullying, assault, mental illness, or any number of other issues, high schoolers deal with real-life situations every day, and they often struggle to be heard in the most important moments. Some students may find themselves constantly wondering why the adults in their lives don't understand.

I spent some time talking with my dad before writing this chapter. We talked about his perception of my brother and me when we were in high school and how that differed from the ways we perceived ourselves. In this chapter, we'll take a look at the "disconnect" we sometimes experience with our parents, as well as how to bridge that gap.

What is the biggest disconnect you feel between yourself and your parents, teachers, or other adults?

Do you feel like the disconnects you experience are becoming more significant or less apparent as you get older?

FRESHMAN

Getting along with parents

My dad's perception of my freshman year was very different from my own. He saw me wake up in the morning and heard my struggle to find the perfect outfit. He watched as I searched for my scattered homework papers and made my lunch as I grabbed a quick breakfast before hurrying out the door for school.

From his point of view, it was easy to see a happy-go-lucky student who spent most of her time worrying about making good grades and fitting in. He was supportive of me in every-thing, always encouraging me to do my best and achieve more than I believed I could. Despite his best intentions, though, there were times when he seemed oblivious to what was really going on in my life.

For me, freshman year was a pretty tumultuous time. I was reeling from the culture shock of a new school, from the aftermath of moving to a new place, and from family changes that forced me to learn new coping skills. During that time, I developed debilitating panic attacks from the stress of juggling so many different things. When I went to my parents seeking help, conversations often ended in "Just relax; you're too hard on yourself." If they were paying attention to me, I thought, they would understand that it wasn't so simple.

Fortunately, by the end of freshman year, I had begun to figure things out. After adjusting to high school, making a few friends, and learning the layout of my new home, I found that some of the stress subsided. My parents and I learned to communicate more effectively with one another and managed to make it through the changes. Even then, however, we didn't always see eye to eye.

So, why the disconnect? I realize now that my parents weren't ignoring what was happening in my life. They were doing their best to connect with me in the midst of changes in their own lives. In reality, my parents and I didn't mean to ignore or belittle each other. The truth was that we were all wrapped up in maintaining our own lives. Let's face it – that can be a struggle at any age.

My parents and I have always been very close, and since my high school years, we've learned to listen and understand each other through trial and error. None of us is perfect, and we still sometimes miss the mark, but we try to keep learning.

In the end, realizing that we were all doing our best, and then deciding to give each other the benefit of the doubt, made a tremendous difference in our relationships with each other. When we stopped focusing on our different perceptions and started considering how the other person actually felt, our relationships began to improve.

Life Hack:

Parents feel pressure, too

As high school students, it's easy to forget that our parents are also working hard. Even when we can't see it, they're probably dealing with social pressures and work problems just like we are.

At the same time, it's been a while since most of our parents were in high school. They may have forgotten how stressful it is. Also, it's not completely their fault when they don't understand the added pressures and expectations that result from increased technology and communication.

As a freshman, it can be easy to discount your parents as insensitive or uncaring, but in reality, they'd probably love to know more about your life. Remember, with practice and a lot of understanding on both sides, it is possible to bridge the gap and fix the disconnect.

Reflection _____ questions for freshmen

Do you feel like you are growing closer to or further away from your parents, grandparents, and/or other trusted adults as you grow older?

What is something you could do to help the important adults in your life understand some of the struggles you face?

SOPHOMORE

Dealing with rules

During my sophomore year, things started to come together for me. After a period of adjustment, my life was finally settling down, and it was easier to take a breath and relax once in a while. This was also the year I turned sixteen, got my drivers' license, and really started pushing back against my parents in a number of ways.

Now that I had become an "expert" at high school, I felt ready for more. I wanted to stay out later with friends, drive myself around on weekends, and go on dates. I had shown my parents I was responsible, and I was frustrated when they wouldn't always give me the freedom I thought I'd earned.

This was especially true of driving with friends. After I received my drivers' license, my parents made a rule that I could only drive one other person in my car for the first year.

As a sophomore, I thought the rule was totally unfair, because I had two friends with whom I spent a significant amount of time. I was the only one of the three of us with access to both a license and a car, but I still couldn't drive both friends anywhere, thanks to my parents' rule.

I argued against the rule constantly, feeling a little hurt and confused about why my parents didn't trust me to drive more than one person at a time. Not only was it an annoying rule that made going out with friends unnecessarily inconvenient, it felt like my parents didn't think I was competent enough to keep myself and my friends safe behind the wheel of a car.

It took a few years (and watching a younger sibling learn

to drive) for me to fully understand their reasoning behind this rule. What I had perceived as distrust was actually concern for my safety. My parents, who had several more years of driving experience than I did, could see I was still figuring out the rules of the road. They knew that having too many friends in the car could be distracting. Furthermore, I had no idea how expensive it could be to fix a wrecked car or pay for insurance following an accident.

A few years down the road (no pun intended), I can see that the rule wasn't about my competence or driving ability as much as it was about preventing a situation that could lead to an accident. As promised, when I had a bit more driving experience, my parents blessed my first three-person excursion.

An important lesson I learned in high school was to think about the other person's intentions when I got into an argument with a friend or family member. For the most part, it's safe to assume your parents aren't setting rules just to be mean to you. After all, seeing you upset is no fun for them either.

By the same token, we hope our parents and friends choose to assume the best about us when we disagree with them. In this case, if my parents had assumed the worst – that I was complaining just for fun – they might have taken away more privileges. In reality, though, they assumed I was upset about the rule for a legitimate reason and, in the end, gave me the freedom I was asking for when they felt it was appropriate.

The disconnect between ourselves and our parents is often perpetuated when we assume the worst of each other. Looking forward, the next time you feel like your parents or another authority figure is giving you a hard time, try to think about the reasoning behind their actions rather than focusing on "winning" the argument.

Life Hack:
Take a deep breath

It's easy to assume the world is against you when a disagreement arises. The next time you find yourself in a disconnected situation, let me suggest that you take a deep breath, step back, and do your best to consider the other person's perspective.

In the long run, even if you still disagree, it will help you to see the other side of things. You'll also be that much closer to finding a solution that works for both of you.

Reflection _____ questions for sophomores

It's easy to believe that adults don't understand our problems. How often, though, do we consider their concerns? What are some issues you have observed the important adults in your life dealing with recently?

When have you disagreed with someone about something you felt strongly about, only to realize later that you might not have been on the right side of the argument after all?

JUNIOR

Finding your own way

My junior year was the first time I heard the question "What do you want to do after high school?" At seventeen, I had no idea what I wanted to do or be when I grew up.

My parents, on the other hand, had several ideas about what they wanted me to be. My mom frequently sent me magazine articles and Facebook posts about the medical field, particularly nursing. "It's a growing industry," she told me, "and you're great with people!"

My dad, on the other hand, wasn't as concerned about my major as he was about what school I attended. He began to casually drop hints about how much fun he'd had in college. He even talked the vice-president of his alma mater into meeting us for lunch on campus one day, so he, too, could tell me what a great school it was.

If my parents had their way, I knew I would be a nursing student attending my dad's alma mater in the fall; but no matter how hard I tried to convince myself, both the major and the school felt wrong.

I had never met a science textbook I liked. I struggled to pass biology and chemistry as a high school student. On top of that, I didn't like the sight of blood, and the thought of giving someone a shot made me queasy.

My dad's college campus was very pretty, but it was smaller than some I had visited, with only 12,000 students. The college itself reminded me a lot of my high school, and there wasn't much to do in the area either. The school had a couple of strong programs, neither of which I was particularly interested in, and, at the end of the day, I knew it just wasn't for me.

When the time came to submit college applications at the end of my junior year, I was conflicted. Should I do what my parents wanted? After all, they had gotten me this far and hadn't steered me wrong yet. Well, not too much, anyway.

On the other hand, I couldn't stop thinking about another school that was much closer to home, with very affordable tuition. I loved the college's campus and had grown up cheering for its football team. Furthermore, most of my friends had already committed to going there, because its academic programs were some of the best in the state.

In terms of a major, I still wasn't entirely sure what to do, but there were a few options that seemed like they were made for me, all in the field of communications. I loved to write, network, and work creatively in groups, and the communications programs seemed to be a great fit for me.

Post-high-school-graduation plans were the first decisions I'd ever made that blatantly went against what my parents had in mind for me. I was uncomfortable with the idea of disappointing my parents, and I worried a lot about what they would think when they learned of my final decision.

I'd like to say they were both immediately happy for me, accepted my decision as final, and supported my academic goals from that moment forward, but that's not exactly how it went.

To clarify, my parents were eventually very happy and supportive, but it took a little while. I stuck to my guns, though, and finally convinced them this was the right choice for me.

Life Hack:

Pleasing everyone isn't always possible

At this point you might be a little confused. Didn't I just tell you in the Sophomore section to consider other people's intentions and to focus on understanding rather than disagreeing? Yes, I did, and that hasn't changed. Bear with me while I explain what I mean.

In terms of your safety or well-being, it's important to listen to your parents. If they have a different opinion than you, listen and do your best to understand where they're coming from. It's generally safe to assume your parents and close friends have your best interests at heart in most situations.

Some decisions, however, you have to make for yourself. Before finalizing my college plans, I thought about my mom and dad's perspectives. I knew they had the best of intentions as they gave me advice. My mom wanted to make sure I chose a field that would prepare me to find a good job, and my dad just wanted to share his enthusiasm for his alma mater with me, so I could enjoy college as much as he had.

Even so, only I could know what college or major was truly right for me, and, at the end of the day, it was up to me to make the final decision. Although it wasn't the school my dad had in mind, I chose a college that was affordable, close to home, and academically strong, which made him happy in the long run. In the same way, although I decided not to

136

become a nursing major, I picked a path in a growing career field, doing work I enjoy, which is ultimately what my mom really wanted.

The truth is that you won't be able to make decisions that please everyone. In the end, the most important thing is that you make safe and healthy choices. Also, in disagreements with people you care about, it's important that you consider the other side of the argument before choosing what you believe is right for you.

You won't always be able to work through your disconnects right away, but over time, it will become easier to bridge the gap and establish your own identity.

Reflection _____ questions for juniors

Have you talked with members of your family about your ideas for life after high school? Do you usually agree or have differences of opinion when you have talks about serious issues?

What is something you can do to make conversations with these adults less argumentative and more constructive?

SENIOR

Reality finally strikes

During my senior year, I felt the effects of being disconnected like never before. The last year of high school was a rush of spending time with friends, getting ready for post-high school life, sending out graduation invitations, packing for college, and – boom – all of a sudden, it was over. I was walking across the stage to receive my high school diploma when I realized I wasn't ready! I had been so busy rushing to get to the end that it hadn't felt real until the moment it was over.

When I remember my senior year, I think of it in two separate parts. The first part was most of the year, having fun with friends, running the school, feeling like a big fish in a small pond, and getting ready for graduation.

The second part was graduation day, when it finally hit me that high school was finished. It was at that moment I wanted to turn around, run back into the building, and refuse to leave my comfort zone ever again.

I can hardly imagine how confused my parents must have been after spending almost a full year hearing "I can't wait to go to college," "I'm so excited to be done with high school," blah, blah, blah ... only then to see me do a complete 180° turn.

Now, a few years removed from high school, I have a better understanding of the disconnect I was feeling with my parents.

In my way of thinking, I had felt ready to be finished with high school for the majority of the year. As the last week grew closer, I could feel senioritis growing stronger with each passing minute. Assignments were tedious, classes were long, and I already had one foot out the door.

But the clock was ticking for my parents, too. My senior year was frustrating for them because it meant I was never home. After school, I was always spending time with friends, going to ball games, or participating in extracurricular activities. My parents, however, were painfully aware of a fact I had completely ignored thus far. They understood that they had only a short time left with me before I took off on my own.

This led to a lot of arguments toward the end of my senior year. Basically, my parents wanted me to spend more time with them, while I wanted to spend as much time as possible with my friends before graduation.

If you're a high school senior and you're wrestling with some of these same things, I have one piece of advice. Think about all the ways you spend your time and decide which of them are most and least important to you. Then, talk to your parents and find out if they are stressed about their lack of time with you.

With any luck, you'll end up meeting in the middle, finding a compromise that works for both of you. If it's as simple as spending an afternoon or two at home during the week and making sure to have dinner with your parents on Mondays and Thursdays, that's easy enough. Put a reminder in your calendar and show up.

Try to make plans with your family that aren't likely to get bumped for other social engagements, and learn to say "no" to going out with friends during times you already have plans with your parents. If you can manage to compromise, your senior year will be much smoother and a lot more fun. Plus, when all is said and done, you'll be so glad you chose to spend time with your family as well as with your friends.

On the flip side, if you're a parent whose high school senior is never home, I have the same piece of advice for you. I know it must be incredibly difficult to let go of the days when your children were always around and dependent on you for everything, but the truth is that senior year is very busy and demanding.

It is quite reasonable to request an evening or two a week for family dinner nights, however. Making these a weekly priority will not only ensure that you see your child during the week, it will also help to maintain a regular schedule instead of trying to keep up with the last-minute planning style of a high school senior.

Talk to your family about picking a couple of nights during the week when everyone can plan to be home. Some of my friends had family game nights; others went out for dinner once or twice a week; and several friends stayed home with their parents and helped cook dinner. Choose what works best for your family and make it part of your regular routine.

If your senior year is like mine was, you may begin to feel a little differently toward the end of the year. The attitude of being "top dog" changes when you realize you're about to start all over again in a new school or job, and it's easy to change your tune about post-grad life.

During this transitional stage, it's okay to stick a little closer to your family and friends. It can be comforting to spend time in familiar places with familiar people.

Even so, know that everything will most likely be just fine after high school. It might be a challenge and a lot to take in at first, but these growing pains are definitely something you can overcome.

Life Hack:

Bear with your parents

Bear with your parents during your senior year, and remember that they're also trying to figure everything out. After all, it's scary for them to see you becoming a full-fledged adult, and it may take them a while to warm up to the idea of you flying the coop.

At the end of the day, patience and communication are the keys to overcoming the "disconnect" during your senior year. Be honest with your parents about what you want and how you're feeling, and then listen and seek to understand them when they talk to you.

More than anything else, just enjoy your senior year. This is what you've worked so hard for; now it's your turn to take on the world. As you read the next chapter, remember how much you've already accomplished and be proud of yourself.

Reflection

If you were grading yourself, how would you rate yourself on a scale of 1 to 10? Mark an X on the line where you would rate yourself.

1 ————————————————————— 10

NO
SENIORITIS

HORRIBLE CASE
OF SENIORITIS

What is something you can do to ease your parents' transition as you grow closer to full-fledged adulthood?

What are some priorities you'd like to focus your time on as a senior?

All Grades

Reflection _____ questions for everyone

Read Ephesians 4:29-32

[29]Do not let any unwholesome talk come out of your mouths, but only what is helpful for building others up according to their needs, that it may benefit those who listen. [30]And do not grieve the Holy Spirit of God, with whom you were sealed for the day of redemption. [31]Get rid of all bitterness, rage and anger, brawling and slander, along with every form of malice. [32]Be kind and compassionate to one another, forgiving each other, just as in Christ God forgave you.

What have you said in recent conversation that might be considered "unwholesome talk"?

Could it be considered a form of unwholesome talk when you argue with family members?

How could arguing with your parents or other family members "grieve the Holy Spirit of God"? What do you think the writer of Ephesians meant by that?

If you took Verses 31-32 more seriously, how would that affect the way you carry on conversations with important adults in your life?

A Word From Zach

The student-parent relationship may be one of the toughest parts of high school, although it may have been a little easier for me because I was the younger sibling.

I think I was probably lucky because my parents had been through this high school parenting thing once before. They knew some of the struggles I would face in the upcoming grades, and I don't think they were as surprised as they probably were when Ashley went through them.

One of my hardest high school struggles was the disconnect between me and my parents at times. Fortunately, it seems like there was no permanent damage. We're getting along better than ever these days.

My advice: Be patient with your parents. Hopefully, they'll be patient with you.

Chapter 8

It's the End of the World
as You Know It
(and you'll be fine)

Primer

How did this happen so quickly? You've made it to the end of this book, and before too long, you will have survived one more year of high school. Depending on when you're reading this, you may be months away or days away, but either way, it's a good bet that you actually will make it through this school year.

Hopefully, as you've read through this book, you've picked up a few helpful tips. Perhaps communication with your parents has improved, or you've found a way to get along with that teacher who just didn't seem to like you.

Regardless of your situation, life keeps on happening. You may soon face a whole new set of changes and find yourself wondering, "So, what now?"

Several times throughout this book, you've been asked to consider some of the challenges you have faced in high school. Thinking back over what you've been through, would you say you're facing more challenges now or fewer than you were a few months ago?

What are some of the challenges you are facing right now?

FRESHMAN

Faith and determination will get you through

High school isn't always easy, especially freshman year. As I told you in Chapter 1, I still remember the stress of finding a seat in the cafeteria during my first week of high school. There were more than 2,000 students in my school, and I knew only a few of them.

Thankfully, there were some kids from my youth group in my high school; otherwise, I would have known only one other freshman, a fellow student from my middle school. You may have had plenty of friends from middle school who entered high school with you, so your transition may have been very different than mine. Or, like I did, you may have transferred from another area of town or moved from another city. Either way, your freshman year can be an exciting–and scary–time.

If you take away just one thing from this book, I hope it's the understanding that faith and determination will get you through just about anything. If you're like most freshmen, you will find that each year of high school gets a little bit easier. That knowledge can definitely help you through the tough times.

I can't overemphasize the importance of leaning on your church family when things get tough. Whether it's problems at school or work, a family situation that seems out of control, or something else, remember the church can help keep you grounded even when things get really tough.

Life Hack:

Double-up on church

Your freshman year is also a time to "double-up" on your church activities. It's tempting to participate less in church activities during high school. However, if you resolve to keep that from happening, you may be the spark that leads others to grow in their faith during their high school years.

You've made it this far. Don't give up. Your future holds so many promises.

Reflection _____ questions for freshmen

What are some of the hardest parts of being a high school freshman?

Who are some older students (sophomores, juniors, or seniors) that you look up to at school, church, or home?

What is it about these older students that causes you to look up to them?

SOPHOMORE

Hold tightly to your faith

I hope you are enjoying your sophomore year. I found it to be much less stressful than the experience of being a new freshman or that of being an upperclassman, having the pressure of taking college entrance exams and preparing for graduation. But life isn't exactly the same for any of us. You may find sophomore year to be a struggle.

Whatever the case may be, hold tightly to your faith. It's easy to pull back from family and faith as you move through high school, but remember, those freshmen are watching you. This is the perfect time to set an example at school and at church.

Remember what it felt like to be a freshman? It hasn't been that long for you. Sophomores seemed so mature and wise. Now, to the new freshman, you're the one who seems mature and wise.

You can make such a difference in the lives of those around you – your family, your friends, and even those younger freshmen at school and church.

Life Hack:

Make this year count

My advice for you is to make this year count! Enjoy each experience. Bask in the glow of knowing your sophomore year can be a great year for you. Enjoy your family and friends. Make extra time for those you love. The next few years will fly by.

Reflection questions for sophomores

Who have you influenced this year? In a good way or a bad way?

What could you do to be a positive, healthy influence on younger students at school or church?

JUNIOR

Your value is not related to your test score

If it's early in the school year, you're already hearing about the standardized tests you'll be taking this year. I took these tests several times, improving my score a little each time. In the end, I had improved significantly. That might not sound like much, but when it came time to pay for college, it was the difference between taking out a big student loan and having much of my education paid for by scholarships.

If I had it to do over, though, I wouldn't stress so much about those tests. They're just tests. You can take them multiple times to improve your score.

Your value as a person is not related to your score on a test. That's not who you are. Remember, we serve a God who values us more than we can ever comprehend. Try to focus on that when you start to get down on yourself.

Life Hack:

Some last minute advice

You've almost made it. Senior year is just ahead, but enjoy your junior year to the fullest. It's almost time for adulthood. Remember to make time for your family. You may still live with them after high school or you may not. Either way, you'll look back and regret the time you didn't spend together while you had the opportunity.

Make your family and your church top priorities. Don't let your faith slide as you move closer to your senior year. This is a time when too many high school students get busy with so many things that they allow their faith to become much less of a priority.

Hold on tightly. You've made it this far. Your future looks amazing.

Reflection_____ questions for juniors

Take a moment to think about your faith. Have you slipped backward or moved forward in your faith journey since entering high school?

List three things you can do to make sure you are moving forward in your faith as you move closer to the end of high school.

SENIOR

You're not done yet

I know you're thinking a lot about the future. The truth is that this isn't the first or the last time you'll anxiously anticipate what's coming next in your life. As a high school senior, I often found myself thinking about what life after high school would mean for me.

In times like these, when it seems like the world as you know it is ending, it's important to remember how far you've already come.

Think back on this year, your senior year of high school. Remember the days when you wondered if you'd be able to get up in the morning, much less make it until the final bell? Somehow, you made it through all of those days, and you'll make it through all of the upcoming changes and new experiences, too.

Whatever the next phase of your life may be, keep in mind that there are many challenges and opportunities ahead. You're not done yet. There are still many things to learn, friends to meet, obstacles to overcome, and victories to be won. This may be the end of the world as you know it, but it's also the beginning of a new adventure.

I remember the end of my senior year. It was a great time, catching up with friends, visiting family, and slacking off in class the week before graduation. At the time, I was so caught up in the rush of graduation parties and family dinners that it never occurred to me to stop and think ... *what's next?*

That was why I found myself completely unprepared the

day I moved into my college dorm. Following the excitement of my senior year, it was intimidating to be back at the bottom of the totem pole, learning the ropes all over again.

During my first few weeks as a college freshman, I was anxious and lonely, feeling like everyone else had already figured out this college thing, while I was still struggling to make ramen noodles in my dorm room. Several times I called my mom at 2:00 a.m., begging her to pick me up and take me home. One particularly rough week, I even considered dropping out of school altogether, unsure I would ever be able to make the adjustments required to succeed in college.

Several weeks later, though, it started getting easier. I could wake up, feed myself, go to class, and finish my homework without too much trouble. I picked up some extracurricular activities and joined a student ministry, which has been one of the best decisions I've ever made in college.

Little by little, I learned my way around, and within a few months, I realized I was legitimately happy. The truth about change is that sometimes it's very difficult. It can be difficult for a long time. Day by day, though, if you stand firm in your faith, it does get easier.

Life Hack:
A new journey awaits you

Yes, your upcoming high school graduation may be the end of the world as you know it, but it's also the beginning of a fantastic new journey. Don't worry, and for now, just enjoy being a high school senior. Work through the hard times, pray a lot, eat good food, lean on friends and family, and, at the end of the day, be proud of yourself and all you've accomplished. Your senior year is literally the adventure of a lifetime, so enjoy every minute of it.

What then? Well, go jump into your next new adventure, whatever it may be. Remember that it's just another season of life, and it will pass, too, just like the others have. Before too long, you'll figure out each new phase of your life, and, hopefully, you'll enjoy each one as much as (or even more than) the last.

Reflection _____ questions for seniors

What scares you the most about life after high school?

What excites you the most about life after high school?

Name an adult whom you can trust and talk to freely when you face difficulties in life.

Name someone who looks up to you as an older, more mature example.

Reflection

Read John 1:9-13

[9] The true light that gives light to everyone was coming into the world. [10] He was in the world, and though the world was made through him, the world did not recognize him. [11] He came to that which was his own, but his own did not receive him. [12] Yet to all who did receive him, to those who believed in his name, he gave the right to become children of God – [13] children born not of natural descent, nor of human decision or a husband's will, but born of God. (NIV)

Who was the light that came into the world?

What is God's promise to those who receive Him?

What does that say about your potential?

As you move ahead in your high school journey, what are some ways in which you can avoid the darkness and grow ever closer to the light?

A Word From Zach

High school might be the time of life when you and your surroundings change the most. However, that doesn't mean you can't make it through successfully.

Just remember, every student in that building has felt awkward and nervous at one time. You're not alone.

Also keep in mind that every person's life is about to change. While the upcoming challenges might seem scary, you will be better equipped to face them because of the struggles you've already worked through.

Chapter 9
Now Get Going!

I began this adventure as a way to help my little brother navigate the sometimes-stormy waters of high school. When I first created my private blog, *Sibling Survival Guide,* I never imagined anyone but my brother would ever read it.

Hopefully, some of what I've shared has been helpful. High school and college turned out to be awesome experiences for me, and it's my hope that you will enjoy your high school years just as much as I did.

I couldn't have done this without Zach. He's a great brother, and I'm starting to think he has loved his high school years even more than I did.

My final advice: Enjoy your high school years. They only come around once.

And keep the faith. Growing up doesn't mean growing away from God. If you remember that, my work is done.

Ashley

Join Ashley's blog at:

marketsquarebooks.com/ashleyconnerblog